W9-DHW-374

To the children of Mithun.

Copyright © 2008 by Ecotone Publishing

All rights reserved. No part of this publication may be reproduced, distributed or transmitted in any
form or by any means, including photocopying, recording, or other electronic or mechanical methods,
without the prior written permission of the publisher, except in the case of brief quotations embodied
in critical reviews and certain other noncommercial uses permitted by copyright law. For permission
requests, write to the publisher, addressed "Attention Permissions Coordinator," at the address below.

For more information write:

Ecotone Publishing
3187 Point White Drive NE
Bainbridge Island, WA 98110

Author: David Macaulay
Book Design: Erin Gehle, softfirm
Edited by: Fred McLennan

Library of Congress Control Number: 2008934277
Library of Congress Cataloging-in Publication Data

ISBN 978-0-9749033-9-2

1. Architecture   2. Design   3. Environment

First Edition

Printed in Canada on Reincarnation Matte paper · one hundred percent recycled content, Processed
Chlorine-Free, using vegetable-based ink.

TABLE OF CONTENTS

ABOUT ECOTONE PUBLISHING

THE GREEN BUILDING PUBLISHER

Ecotone Publishing - exploring the relationship between the built and natural environments

Founded and operated by green building experts, Ecotone Publishing is the first book publisher to focus solely on green architecture and design. Headquartered on Bainbridge Is., WA, the company is dedicated to meeting the growing demand for authoritative and accessible books on sustainable design, materials selection and building techniques in North America and beyond. Ecotone institutes a variety of green strategies, including the printing of its books on recycled content paper with vegetable-based inks, the use of recyclable packaging and supporting employees telecommuting from home offices. Ecotone proudly supports environmental and social organizations through collaboration, partnership and membership. An industry leader, Ecotone is the first American publishing company to fully adopt carbon neutrality to its business practices, in order to offset its own contributions to climate change.

Our commitment to the environment and to a sustainable future is the driving force behind every action we undertake.

www.ecotonedesign.com

ECOTONE AND MITHUN

Ecotone Publishing is dedicated to spreading the word about important subjects, projects and people that are vital to a sustainably-designed world. Through this book, we are very proud to share the enlightenment, the achievements and profound connections to nature that Mithun celebrates through its exemplary practice. We hope that readers of *Integrated Design – MITHUN* will derive a deeper understanding of responsible landscape architecture, architecture and interior design and that inspiration and thoughtful action will result.
The people at Ecotone extend a heartfelt thank you to the highly talented and dedicated designers at Mithun for their collective generosity of time and the sharing of information. The professional collaboration between Ecotone and Mithun has been truly enjoyable and fruitful.

COLOPHON

Reflecting the environmental ethos of Ecotone, we selected environmentally-responsible materials for the production of this book. Reincarnation Matte paper is one hundred percent recycled, manufactured from fifty percent Post-Consumer Waste fiber (PCW), is Process Chlorine Free (PCF) and utilizes electricity that is offset with Green-e® certified renewable energy certificates. Reincarnation Matte paper is ancient forest friendly. Utilization reduces solid waste from entering landfill sites, and uses less water in manufacturing than conventional paper, decreasing air and water pollution. Ecotone also chose vegetable-based ink to compliment the paper selection. Compared to petroleum inks, vegetable-based inks release less than twenty percent of the mass of volatile organic chemicals and are more readily recycled.

ENVIRONMENTAL BENEFITS STATEMENT

ECOtone Publishing LLC saved the following resources by printing the pages of this book on chlorine free paper made with 50% post-consumer waste.

TREES	WATER	ENERGY	SOLID WASTE	GREENHOUSE GASES
15	5,643	11	934	1,721
FULLY GROWN	GALLONS	MILLION BTUs	POUNDS	POUNDS

Calculations based on research by Environmental Defense and the Paper Task Force. Manufactured at Friesens Corporation

ACKNOWLEDGEMENTS

David R. Macaulay

It has been an amazing journey: to explore the world of Mithun Inc., to gain a unique behind-the-scenes look at some of the greenest built places on the planet. Landscapes that blend art, science and native environments. Plans to create urban districts and neighborhoods designed to perform like pristine Northwest forests. Structures filled with light and color, informed by water, energy and earth. With each new project completed and those still on the boards, I remain in awe, inspired again and again, by the concepts, the honest detail and the passion that continues to drive the firm's growing body of work.

Over the last two years, I have been privileged to spend a great deal of time with Mithun staff, "Mithunees" they like to call themselves – much of it at the firm's incredible Pier 56 offices, while gaining a first-hand look at an array of buildings, landscapes and communities in and around Seattle, Denver and elsewhere. In particular, my deepest gratitude goes to Bert Gregory, FAIA, Mithun's CEO and president, for his insights on the firm's ongoing evolution, his rich storytelling, and especially his positive vision on what the future holds as the world begins to seriously address place-making, community building, and living and restorative design on a scale never imagined before.

A very special thanks also goes to Mithun principals Dave Goldberg, Deb Guenther and Rich Franko. Their input was invaluable while guiding my understanding of the design moves and principles that have resulted in so many award-winning projects: IslandWood, High Point, Zoomazium, Epler Hall, Lloyd Crossing, the REI flagships and counting. Mithun's marketing team played an incredibly important role as well – focusing and shaping Integrated Design-MITHUN, keeping us on track, offering critical perspectives on the culture, practices and projects of the firm. Curt Pliler, Mithun's Director of Brand, has been our point person at Mithun, expertly facilitating the flow of information and responsible for an incredible array of photographs and images that illustrate this book. Charles Moss, Mithun, for producing the compelling artwork on each Principles page. And Bonnie Duncan, Mithun's Director of Communications, has been a terrific partner with her timely edits and suggestions, offering many valuable ideas to improve the overall narrative of this story.

In addition, I am thankful to my many "tour guides" at Mithun, who generously shared their time and knowledge on site visits that proved vital in crafting the character of this book. With Thom Emrich, Mithun's past president, on a tour of Bellevue, Washington, I gained a deeper appreciation of the history and design traditions of Mithun's early days. T. Frick took me to Taylor 28, a forgotten piece of Seattle's urban fabric being transformed into a completely new, sustainable streetscape. Bill Kreager spent part of a day with us at High Point in West Seattle, an emerging green neighborhood that redefines the meaning of community. Through Ken Boyd's eyes, I was better able to understand the beautiful detail and integrated strategies that make up REI's Seattle Flagship store – the project that, perhaps more than any other, propelled Mithun into the spotlight as a sustainable design leader.

Many more Mithun principals and associates were instrumental as well in conveying the true spirit, design fundamentals and multi-disciplinary practices of the firm – including Ron van der Veen, Brendan Connolly, Sean Cryan, Brodie Bain, Critter Thompson, Paul Wanzer, Laura Curry, Chris Dixon, Kim Munizza, Mike Fowler, Susan McNabb, Jim Bodoia, Steve Cox, and Dan Swaab. Leslie Welshimer, Naoe White, Jason Moll, Angela Minton, Jenny Rose Ryan, Lynn McBride, and Brad Fanta also provided important contacts, edits, images and other essential background materials to complete the firm's portrait.

Integrated Design- MITHUN would not have been possible without Jason F. McLennan, Ecotone's founder and publisher, who believed this Seattle innovator would be the ideal candidate for a new title featuring one of the best and the brightest green design firms in North America. Likewise, Mike Berrisford of Ecotone was our fearless project manager and Fred McLennan our tireless editor. And as always, it has been a pleasure to work with designer Erin Gehle on what is again an appealing, elegant addition to the literature of green architecture.

Finally, I would like to thank my friends and family, both the Macaulays and the Bridges, for their love, patience and support – especially my wife, the poet Lanie Gray, and our kids Eli and Susannah, who continue to surprise and inspire me every day.

FOREWORD

Judith Heerwagen, Ph.D.

Integrated Design – MITHUN is a must read for architects, planners, organizational leaders and others who aspire to create buildings that are sensitive to the environment and wonderful places for people.

There is much talk these days about integrated design, but little understanding of how to actually do it. It's hard. It's messy. It frays the nerves at times. But when it works well, it creates great satisfaction for everyone – from the design team to the client and building occupants. I know this because I had the pleasure to work with a multidisciplinary Mithun team not long ago.

It's the behind-the-scenes work of this group that I would like to talk about here, because this is ultimately what creates a better building. It's the human element at work -- problem solving, debating, clarifying, testing, and laughing. Yes, laughing and joking.

A good integrated team shows the very best features of Homo ludens, the playful human. Playing – whether with ideas or props – is at the heart of creativity and imagination. Playfulness relieves tensions and supports the social bonds that build the sense of trust and intellectual security necessary to work in an integrated manner. As a behavioral psychologist, I was often perplexed by technological discussions. But as a member of the Mithun team, I felt totally comfortable asking for clarification and explanation. The team members felt equally comfortable questioning my assumptions and ideas.

In a multidisciplinary setting, the most difficult challenge is understanding and exploiting different perspectives and knowledge bases. It takes a good dose of patience and mental effort. Yet, without this blended insight, a truly integrated design is impossible. In some ways, integrated design is more like a water color painting than a jigsaw puzzle where there is only one solution and all of the pieces fit together in a pre-determined way. Integrated design is blended and seamless. The concepts and solutions overlap and support one another, rather than fight for dominance. And getting there doesn't happen without a collaborative team where all the voices are heard and where unexpected ideas aren't ridiculed, but rather become the stuff around which real solutions are created.

What you will find in this book are the end products of a Mithun team process that is truly integrated in the full sense of the term. Collaborative, cooperative, willing to ask "what if?," challenging assumptions, breaking out of old habits, learning, teaching, inspiring the best in everyone. And most important, creating buildings and places that are beautiful, ecologically sound, culturally relevant, and wonderful places for living and working.

INTRODUCTION

Bert Gregory, FAIA, Mithun

A few years ago I was invited to a small dinner party to visit with Paul Hawken and learn of his wonderful life and thoughts of the future. It was a great dinner with good wine, and fine conversation.

At the end of the dinner, my host and client from our IslandWood learning center project, Debbi Brainerd, asked each of us, "What gives us hope?"

Debbi and Paul Brainerd each said, "Children give me hope." It was a natural response from a couple who have catalyzed a positive future for the Puget Sound region with their vision to connect children with the natural world. There is, indeed, magic in children asking "why?" and believing that they will be part of the answer.

Denis Hayes of the Bullitt Foundation, a non-profit foundation focused on environmental stewardship, shocked us. He said that his hope was for mankind in the 22nd Century, after environmental issues and nuclear proliferation had run its course.

The table became quiet.

After several moments of silence and a few additional fine comments, Paul Hawken spoke. He said, "My hope is in the realization by individuals that they are part of a global system." Always a futurist, Hawken was sensing the rapid pace of change we are now experiencing — change being driven by awareness.

Somehow I ended up last.

I said, "My hope is in cities and integrated design."

Omer Mithun, the firm's founder, established an inquisitive culture at Mithun in the middle of the 20th Century that endures to this day. This book is as much about the question as it is about the answer. It is about a wonderful group of people believing strongly in the collaborative approach to design, searching for the holistic solution, and integrating disciplines, knowledge and inquiry. It is about seeking spirit as we merge science and design.

Join us now, and as Omer would say, "Pull up a chair." This is a story about people, community, and integrated design. It is about asking "why?" on a journey to create places that are one with nature.

It is about hope.

FIRM MISSION:
Inspiring a sustainable world through leadership,
innovation, and integrated design.

CHAPTER 1:
AT MID-CENTURY, A NEW BEGINNING

"Omer was the conductor of the architectural orchestra that was his practice and his career and teaching. It wasn't so much about being an architectural star; it was more about conducting others. And just as a major component of being a conductor is about the practice as much as the performance, that's what Omer was about, too: teaching, helping others become the best voices they could become."

—*Thom Emrich, AIA, Mithun*

FOUNDED IN A DESIRE TO TEACH, CURIOUS, INNOVATIVE, DEFINING A NEW ARCHITECTURE

"It seems that laughter needs an echo."
—*Henri Bergson*

Seattle, like the rest of post-war America, was hungry for the new architectural designs sparked by a building boom sweeping across the country. Here and across the Pacific Northwest, the economy and a growing population had attracted a crop of young, talented architects eager to experiment, to change the environment of everyday life through design. These new arrivals included names such as Ibsen Nelsen, Fred Bassetti, A.O. Bumgardner, Paul Thiry and Omer Mithun.

City suburbs in a wide open landscape, the spaces between, so full of potential it would be the focus of most of the region's architects after the war. That meant unprecedented demand for residential design as well as suburban churches, libraries, schools and clinics. For Omer Mithun and his new company, that potential would be realized east of Seattle in Bellevue, named one of eleven "All America" cities in 1955. It was here the firm began to earn a reputation for genuineness and creativity, known for the passion, technical competence, vision and collaborative spirit of its designers. Here, too, more than fifty years ago, the firm started to shape a path toward sustainable design: built on the legacy of Mithun's Nordic heritage and expressing such values as clarity of form, innovation and a connection with nature.

THE "GLASS BANK" & OTHER STORIES
The son of Norwegian immigrants, a Midwesterner and Naval architect during World War II, Omer Mithun opened his own architecture practice in downtown Bellevue, Washington in 1949. Incorporated in 1953, the city was expanding rapidly with huge subdivisions of ranch and contemporary homes; by 1954 people were talking about the new "gracious living" just east of Seattle. Mithun would design many homes in Bellevue's Surrey Downs neighborhood,

GLASS BANK, 1956: Mithun's earliest example of solar design, the lobby of the Washington State Bank Building relied on a careful calculation of shadows and deep fins on the curtain wall to protect interior spaces from the sun. It was known nationally as the "Glass Bank" and earned an AIA Award of Merit for the firm.

including the Lurie House (1952). Life here, with its curved streets, natural landscaping and wide lots, gave residents the impression they were deep within a northwest forest setting while only a few minutes drive from downtown Seattle. During this time, the practice offered both architecture and planning services, hinting at its broader, integrated design work to come later.

As Bellevue and the Eastside grew, Mithun's firm would diversify with new residential neighborhoods, corporate offices, medical office buildings, municipal offices, churches, fire and police stations, and shopping centers. Its designs garnered 1955 AIA Seattle Honor Awards for the Medical Arts Center (Bellevue) and Washington State Bank (Mercer Island). The Strandberg Residence in Bellevue was recognized as the Seattle Times/AIA Home of the Year in 1955. That same year, Mithun would become architect of record for the First Presbyterian Church of Bellevue, a relationship that has lasted for more than fifty years and eighteen additions.

The mid-1950s were also a period when Mithun began to experiment with passive solar heating and cooling through its design of the Washington State Bank Building (1956) in Bellevue. This International Style building featured a green glass curtain wall on three sides (north, south and east), utilizing deep fins to protect interior spaces from solar gain. The flat roof also retained a one-inch film of water as an insulator and to reflect the sun. For its elegant, radically-new design concepts, the "Glass Bank" won an AIA Award of Merit in 1958 and was highlighted in both *Time Magazine* and *Architectural Forum*.

After a series of partners and company names, Omer Mithun settled in as the leader of Mithun & Associates. While it remained

relatively small, the practice would increasingly inform his work at the university, just as the university teaching would inform the practice's designs. More AIA Seattle awards went to Mithun for Bellevue projects that included the Weeks Residence (1959), First Presbyterian Church of Bellevue (1959) and The Village (1968), along with College Place Medical Center in Lynnwood, Washington (1969).

EVERWOOD

Into the 1970s, much of Mithun's architecture reflected and refined the Northwest Contemporary style, a regional variant of Modernism popular around Seattle and Portland. The design of Bellevue's Sahalee Village Condominiums (1973 AIA Honor Award) was also influenced by the emerging energy crisis. As a result, the buildings feature early passive solar designs and thermal massing elements to collect and store heat. Mithun was recognized as well for Lockwood Townhomes (1974 AIA Commendation), a site-sensitive development that integrated homes among the trees overlooking Meydenbauer Park in Bellevue.

Mithun's new work space went further still with these energy- and environment-inspired ideas. Located across Bellevue in the just-completed Everwood Office Park, the new Mithun Associates Office (1975 AIA First Honor Award) took advantage of natural daylighting and solar orientation, set in the midst of trees and creating a secluded feel within a suburban context. Naturally cooled, its mostly wood interiors with exposed trusses, many windows and open work spaces were strikingly similar to Mithun's later Pier 56 and San Francisco offices.

The Mithun Associates (as it was now known) continued to garner AIA Seattle awards regularly for the firm's innovative designs on the Eastside. Green design sensibilities were becoming more evident as well. The recreation building (1977) for Sammamish Townhomes northeast of Bellevue was Mithun's first design of a green roof. A new solar greenhouse for the Overlake School (1978) in Redmond featured south-facing windows and overhead plexiglass panels to collect sunlight. Designers also experimented with thermal storage, utilizing a thick concrete wall in-between the greenhouse and the north side of the building (the science classroom) to store heat during the day and release it at night.

The firm also worked on a series of passive solar houses, beginning with the APA Sun House (1978) in Bellevue – designed to cut heating costs in half using "a system that's simple, clean and highly efficient," observed Omer Mithun. The next year Mithun was invited to design a demonstration active solar house for Washington Natural Gas in Kirkland, Washington. This single-family residence (1982), tracked by NASA computers for the first year, features an active solar energy system to supply space heating and domestic hot water.

Throughout the 1980s, Mithun continued to shape Bellevue's central business district and design several city landmarks. The firm also specialized in health care facilities, city halls for small municipalities and especially residential projects. Notable design work included Corporate Campus East, a seven-building office park (1981 to 1987) that became the original Microsoft campus, and City Limits (1982) near Bellevue's emerging downtown. A precursor to the environmentally-smart, high-density housing that would become central to Mithun's practice, City Limits was designed as a series

of two-story urban courtyard town homes arranged on an east-west axis with passive heat supplement. Town home windows, facing south onto a private landscaped court, gathered the warmth of the sun in the winter, with solar shades protecting interior spaces in the summer. The north wall of one unit became the private courtyard wall of another.

On March 23, 1983, Omer L. Mithun – founder, mentor, teacher, and civic leader – passed away after a long battle with cancer. Later that year, the practice became Mithun Bowman Emrich Group with Thom Emrich as president and J. Don Bowman as chairman. The firm was concerned about the possible loss of clientele that Mithun had personally built over thirty years. So to further protect and strengthen its client base across a variety of markets, top management invited several architects as new owners, each with a different project area or technical expertise. In 1988, Mithun Partners was born.

Thirty miles east of Seattle, the Salish Lodge renovation and addition (1988) presented a completely new and very high-profile opportunity for Mithun's designers. This historic mountain retreat overlooking Snoqualmie Falls had long been a cultural institution, familiar to generations of Puget-Sound area families who came for the scenic view and the famous specialty breakfasts. Mithun supervised remodeling of the 1919 lodge structure, which then reopened as the 89-room Salish Lodge & Spa. Meanwhile, the practice was increasingly focused on solutions, as Emrich explained, "'to enliven the environment in some way that goes beyond simply solving the program of the client". [1]

SIGN OF THINGS TO COME: Through the 1950s, 1960s and 1970s, the firm continued to explore Modernism's Northwest Contemporary style – developing solid relationships with area developers and creating Eastside residences known for their scale, detailing and site-sensitive design. The Strandberg House (top) was Seattle Times/AIA Home of the Year for 1955. Bellevue's Lockwood Townhomes (middle) rises out of the trees. A demonstration house (bottom) for Washington Natural Gas was the practice's first to feature active solar technologies.

SCENIC ESCAPE: From food and rest stop to four-star resort, the renowned Salish Lodge next to Snoqualmie Falls has long been one of Washington State's most popular attractions. Designs for the award-winning remodel (1988) and Japanese-style spa addition (1996) stand out in a long tradition of hospitality work at Mithun.

BOOMTOWN: After a decade of phenomenal growth for the city, by 1999 Mithun had become one of the largest architecture practices in Greater Seattle – recently completing a major renovation of the historic Smith Tower for the Samis Foundation (top) and at work on a new corporate campus for SHS.com (bottom) in Anacortes, Washington.

OMER AND TRUBY: The Mithuns at Willapa Bay on the coast of Washington.

"The REI flagship store in Seattle was not only a success for REI, but for the design team as well. All members of the design team collaborated, and 'owned' the conceptual idea. As an interior designer it was an epiphany as I was involved at the outset, working in the most exhilarating, integrated fashion. People were working together, the spaces between team members, sometimes filled with friction, sometimes delight, but the huge creative potential that emerged was incredible. The team had a 'moment' that shaped my belief in the power of integrated thought and design."

—Kim Munizza, IIDA, Mithun

Now, at the end of the decade, Mithun Partners faced one of the most difficult choices in the firm's history. It was the premier practice in Bellevue, clearly identified with the city's growth, and well connected throughout the Eastside. Most importantly, Mithun's management understood that to attract top talent and commissions they needed to be part of an urban Seattle, tied more closely to the environment and design challenges of the city.

They began to look west.

SEATTLE BOUND
In April 1990, Mithun opened its doors for the first time in Seattle. Located in the historic Times Square Building (1915) within the city's Central Business District, the firm's fifty employees moved into the top two floors of this flatiron high-rise at Fifth, Olive and Stewart – in the midst of a retail shopping area and only a few blocks from Seattle's famous Pike Place Market.

The next year brought another boost in Mithun's size and capabilities. A merger with Roger Williams Architects reinforced the growing international focus of the practice, which continued to pursue opportunities in Japan with work on a resort community near Mt. Fuji, as well as smaller projects in Osaka, Kobe and Tokyo. Several staff members also continued a Mithun tradition as instructors at UW's Department of Architecture. Concurrently, Don Bowman retired while Bert Gregory and Bruce Williams stepped into leadership roles. A tradition of professional leadership also began, as both Roger Williams and Thom Emrich served as AIA Seattle presidents in the late 1980s (followed by Bert Gregory in 1998 and Lee Copeland in 2008).

Then came REI. The design of REI's new Seattle Flagship store beginning in 1993 would be transformative in how Mithun approached materials, light, air, temperature and site – building on its tradition of creating spaces with energy and resource efficiency in mind. For Bert Gregory, this project represented the firm's biggest commitment to sustainable design yet: "The REI commission really helped bring focus to our firm. In the early Nineties there wasn't a lot of information out there, but we really got ourselves educated about issues of what it takes to build as responsibly, intelligently, and environmentally sensitive as we could."[2]

Over the next three years, the REI Seattle project would consume much of Mithun's time and attention leading up to the store's grand opening in 1996 – earning a host of honors for the firm locally (1996 AIA Seattle Award of Merit, 1996 AIA Northwest and Pacific Region Honor Award) and nationally (1999 AIA/COTE Top Ten Green). The project would also generate significant new opportunities that included design of REI's Bloomington store (1997), REI corporate headquarters, the retailer's first international store in Tokyo (2000), and a second flagship store in Denver (2001 AIA/COTE Top Ten Green and National Trust for Historic Preservation Honor Award). The broadly integrated nature of projects for REI – combining architecture, planning, interior design, resource systems engineering and landscape architecture – also prompted the firm's leadership to update and clarify the firm's values. Beginning in 1995, and renewed every five years thereafter, Mithun asserted its identity as a principled culture focused on design, sound economics and positive benefit to people, the community and the environment.

OMER MITHUN: "PULL UP A CHAIR, LET'S TALK"

His trademark smile was ever-present, expressing an intense curiosity, and always, his optimism for the future. Omer Mithun was eager to learn, to create change through design. Mostly, he will be remembered as a teacher: a mentor every morning in Mithun's office, his afternoons spent at the University of Washington where he influenced a generation of architects. "Pull up a chair, let's talk", he'd say.

Omer Lloyd George Mithun was born in Marcus, Iowa and raised in Steen, Minnesota, discovering his passion for architecture while at the University of Minnesota. There, he became fascinated with the International Style Modernism of Europe. Soon after the War in the Pacific broke out, he enlisted. The career of Lieutenant Mithun would take him to Washington, DC, to Ann Arbor for a Master's in Naval Architecture, and finally to the Puget Sound Naval Shipyard in Bremerton, Washington. Following the war, he opened his own architecture office in 1949 in Bellevue, a city poised for significant growth at the start of a new decade. The next year, he began a thirty-two-year tenure as a professor and then nearly twenty years as chair of the Bellevue Planning Commission. His practice would remain small during his lifetime – but its reputation for professionalism and quality, consistent design would change the face of suburban King County. In marking the firm's growing influence, Bellevue's Journal-American called him "'Mr. Architect': Omer Mithun gives East Side buildings that belong."

"To describe Omer in two words: infectious enthusiasm. And that is what he displayed every day that I saw him in the office or at the university – there was always something new and interesting and exciting to him. He had a terrific enthusiasm for life. Every day was a great day."

—*Fred Brown, AIA, Mithun*

OMER L. MITHUN, FAIA
June 10, 1918 · March 23, 1983

BA, Architecture, University of Minnesota, 1942
MS, Naval Architecture, University of Michigan, 1945
Established Wilson-Mithun, 1949; then Mithun & Nesland, Mithun,
Ridenour & Cochran, Mithun & Associates, and The Mithun
Associates
Chair, Bellevue Planning Commission 1953-72, and Medina Planning
Commission, 1965-1982
Assistant Professor/Professor, University of Washington, Department
of Architecture, 1950-1982
AIA College of Fellows, 1973

Mithun's much-publicized design of the new Spa at Salish Lodge (1996 AIA Seattle Commendation) also led to a series of commissions for new hotel, spa, conference centers, and golf club projects. The firm doubled in size between 1997 and 1999 to keep up with multiple practice areas and a growing array of commercial, institutional and medical projects. By now, landscape architecture had been added to architecture, urban planning and interior design as Mithun further explored multidisciplinary design approaches within the firm.

In April 1999 alone, Mithun's designers were busy with a corporate campus for SHS.com (Shared Healthcare Systems) along the waterfront in Anacortes, Washington and renovation of the Exchange Building, an historic downtown Seattle high-rise just underway. Design of a new environmental learning center on Bainbridge Island (IslandWood) was on the boards – the first Mithun project utilizing Thermal Analysis Software to drive integrated energy demand reduction through natural cooling and the first to include a Living Machine® and constructed wetlands for integrated water treatment and recycling. Also, extensive renovation of Smith Tower, a 42-story Seattle landmark, was nearing completion. Mithun's residential team was fueling much of this growth while focused on planning, urban infill, new large master planned communities, and specialized senior housing facilities around the country. For its award-winning Victoria Townhomes in Seattle's Queen Anne neighborhood and other accomplishments, Mithun would later earn 2001 "Top Firm" honors from *Residential Architect* magazine.

With nearly one hundred-sixty employees spread across several offices and four floors of the Times Square Building, internal communication was becoming more difficult, the work environment less than ideal. Mithun's leaders knew their future had to be elsewhere; they wanted and needed to stay somewhere within Seattle's city center. That is when they discovered an old, dark, abandoned pier on the waterfront: recognizing its potential to help revitalize a neighborhood and as the perfect place to express Mithun's history, commitment to sustainability and values as an integrated design practice.

By March 2000, the renovation of Pier 56 was complete, resulting in a beautiful, expansive, sustainable space for two hundred employees – naturally daylit, naturally ventilated and filled with views of Puget Sound. That same year, Mithun switched to chlorine-free recycled paper products, eliminated petroleum-based foam core boards, and launched concerted efforts to reduce the firm's environmental impact. Bert Gregory, now a national leader and advocate for sustainable design and urbanism, became Mithun's new president and CEO.

REI CAMPUS: The success of the Seattle Flagship store design led directly to a commission for doubling REI's headquarters campus in Kent, Washington. A new cafeteria, conferencing and auditorium facilities, and a central landscaped courtyard – totaling 165,000 square feet of office and support space – reflect the outdoor retailer's store designs and commitment to sustainability.

OFFICE LIGHT: Mithun's new office space (1974) at Everwood Park on the outskirts of Bellevue proved to be its strongest statement yet of integrated design: daylighting, natural ventilation, passive solar, natural wood interiors and an open work environment – all a clear precursor to the later work of the firm.

PRINCIPLE 1

GROW AN IDEA

CENTER FOR URBAN AGRICULTURE

"This is a new model, a new topology for urban living – something that's critical to helping us explore solutions to climate change as well as clean water and food supply challenges. It's become a touchstone for where all of our projects need to go. Each of these technologies have occurred somewhere – just never all together in one place. I think that's a moment of hope, it really is possible."

—Debra Guenther, ASLA, Mithun

CENTER FOR URBAN AGRICULTURE (CUA)

Seattle, Washington

April 2007

"To live/work/farm: twenty-three stories high"

What began as an intriguing idea – the living building – quickly evolved into a literal exploration of community, affordable housing and sustainability to win "Best of Show" in the Cascadia Region Green Building Council's "Living Building Challenge" for 2007. It is highly conceptual, designed to function like a living organism, and yet deeply rooted in research and rigorous calculations to meet its goals.

The multi-story Center for Urban Agriculture (CUA) is at once a vision of vertical farmland, wildlife habitat, high-rise living, and a laboratory for avoided carbon, biodiversity and energy self-

sufficiency. Totaling 122,000 square feet, the CUA produces nearly 100 percent of its own energy using a 34,000-square-foot PV array, while a neighborhood-wide storm water scheme supplies up to 68 percent of its water needs. The Center reintroduces extensive patches of native plant communities. South-facing greenhouses and rooftop gardens offer an additional 17,600 square feet for food production. The building's 318 residential units (studio and one- and two-bedroom) incorporate retrofitted, recycled shipping containers within its superstructure. As a living building, CUA rises to the challenge: designed to operate elegantly, using resources efficiently and for maximum beauty, inspiring a revolution.

Cultivating, growing, shaping and evolving. Revealing itself over time. No preconceptions, no assumptions. Only questions: open-ended, testing, exploring every possibility. "Grow An Idea", at Mithun, is a defining principle that informs all its other principles, the genesis of a solution. It is listening to the land at night – and later to nine- and ten-year-olds who would some day stay there – that creates the magic of an outdoor education center. Or paying close attention to how a contemporary, mixed-used complex might become a beautiful backdrop for an historic downtown park. And through enhancing the visitor experience, creating a sense of adventure, within a completely new kind of retail environment.

You do not come to the table with a complete concept. You might already have the seed of the idea, or many ideas, but it is important to learn from a program, from a place, from the needs of the client...all those circumstances that inform the project.

Storytelling, integrating art and architecture, the choreography of a space, the sequence of arrival – each an outcome, a response, that relates to place and purpose.

Immersion. Interpretation. Context. For Mithun's designers, these are vital tools and techniques for crafting an entrance, a courtyard, a street corner that mirrors the client's hopes and dreams. All are essential to understanding a site, to capturing its story. Inspiration may come through sketches, journaling, models – even from examining a rock or wildflower during a spring field trip. Finding answers, growing, nurturing the seed of an idea for the next project.

CHAPTER 2:
INSPIRED, EVOLVING: A CULTURE OF POSSIBILITIES

"It is all about communication and teamwork and sharing. We took the best areas within our new office and made them common spaces. That was such a big move, a big part of our culture now. And from a sustainability standpoint: you share daylight, you share ventilation, you share views. It is a space that supports collaboration."

—Dave Goldberg, AIA, Mithun

COMMUNITY, PROCESS, CONTINUOUS LEARNING AND LIFE AT MITHUN

"Once individuals link together they become something different... Relationships change us, reveal us, evoke more from us. Only when we join with others do our gifts become visible, even to ourselves."
Margaret Wheatley and Myron Kellner-Rogers

Corporate culture at Mithun is best summed up by a short, simple declaration found in the firm's strategic plan: "To be a principled culture focused on design." Here is an environment of continuous learning, of cooperation and collaboration, where co-workers share skills and teach each other. Where design excellence means innovation and a passion for the art of design as well as integrated thinking, risk taking and high ethical standards. Where sustainability is central to every project – every building and landscape – and to the practice itself, extending beyond the work at Mithun to families and community.

Work and life intertwine at Mithun: celebrating another new LEED® Accredited Professional or participating in the bi-annual Mithun Olympics. It means taking advantage of frequent learning opportunities, whether a Friday lecture about Scandinavian design or a product lunch on sustainably-harvested wood. It is spirited research that investigates a systems-wide approach to carbon reduction during the Lloyd Crossing Sustainable Urban Design Plan in 2003. Or collaborating with the Lady Bird Johnson Wildflower Center in 2006 to create BuildCarbonNeutral.org, the first online calculator to gauge a project's embodied carbon. And it is sketching a streetscape in Barcelona while on a study trip abroad, signing up for bike-to-work month, and continually offering fresh ideas to make the office a little greener.

Without question, Mithun's renovated warehouse space at Pier 56 exemplifies the vision, the spirit and especially the people of this firm. Its office on Seattle's waterfront is egalitarian, bright, open and airy – as well as productive, adaptable and communicative. Moving into historic Pier 56 in 2000 – from a downtown Seattle office, and before that an office perched

GINGERBREAD HOUSE: When it is time to make gingerbread houses again for charity, architect Antonio Peres and his daughters are ready to pitch in. It is one of many in-house benefits and volunteer opportunities that Mithun staff initiate, a chance to give back, to build community inside and outside Pier 56.

in the trees of Bellevue, Washington – fully expressed Mithun's deep respect for tradition and an intense optimism about the future.

CHANGING THE WORLD, FROM PIER 56

On any given day, a walk through this office of more than two hundred people reveals much about the culture, community and work style of the firm. "Main Street" runs through the heart of the building, depicting Mithun's full range of work: projects built, under construction, and still on the boards. There are models of Seattle's Zoomazium on display, the Teton Science School in Wyoming and the University of Washington's Nordheim Court. Lining most of this central walkway are large posters: a vision plan for a large district in Seattle's south downtown, the Seattle Aquarium, Mosler Lofts, the Denver REI Flagship, redevelopment around the Tacoma waterfront, the Lloyd Crossing concepts for Portland's Pearl District. Further down is "Glimpse," a constantly changing display of sketches and renderings highlighting a current project. Opposite that is Mithun's model shop, where anyone can walk by and see first hand how projects evolve. In the middle of Main Street, the staff gathers every Thursday afternoon for a lively design critique: this week to examine a new environmental education center in Kentucky, next week an eco resort in Arizona.

At the western end of Mithun's office overlooking Elliott Bay and the Olympic Mountains is Point No Point, a common area for collaboration, spontaneous meetings with clients and consultants, or just lunch. After work, it becomes a public space for receptions, lectures and many local non-profits use it. Through the windows and across the water, the view is spectacular: busy with cruise ships, the ferry to Bainbridge Island, giant container ships on their way to

China, and occasionally the sight of seals, otters and blue herons.

To either side of Main Street and filling the pier's second floor are the workspaces. Mithun functions as one office. This office is integrated design in action: where staff members group together into blended teams of architects, interior designers, landscape architects, urban planners, ecologists and other specialties. There is no hierarchy or segregation of disciplines here, no studios or departments, no private offices, walls or partitions. Everyone – from Mithun's president to the newest intern – sits at the same size desk, able to see their neighbors in the next aisle through simple bookcases. This is a project-focused office, physically and organizationally, where the best resources, experience and staff are brought to every opportunity. Because of this focus, every four to six months another set of staff members move, new teams form, and another project is underway.

A FOUNDATION OF VALUES

Mithun's stated mission is to inspire a sustainable world through leadership, innovation and integrated design. This mission involves actively participating in the advancement of sustainable design knowledge worldwide, with equally ambitious goals to make a tangible difference: creating cities, places and spaces that strengthen community, respect global natural systems and elevate the human spirit.

In carrying out its mission, the firm measures success in a variety of ways. As designers, Mithun values the judgment of peers – organizations such as the American Institute of Architects, the American Society of Landscape Architects, and the International Interior Design Association. Projects and corporate operations alike

are evaluated against benchmarks relative to low environmental impact. Through its accounting system, Mithun keeps track of carbon-producing activities, such as air and car travel, gas mileage and use of electricity, and then purchases carbon offsets through the Chicago Climate Exchange and the Bonneville Environmental Foundation. The firm also measures success based on an ability to "give back", balancing annual contributions against revenue. This drive to promote quality of life extends to pro bono work involving local efforts to improve education, the natural environment, and access to civic and cultural experiences. Mithun also regularly partners with non-profits to help them acquire grants aimed at revitalizing local communities in sustainable ways.

Finally, Mithun seeks four main qualities in its team members – "who need to be smart, creative, nice and experienced," says Bert Gregory, Mithun's president and CEO since 2000. "The first three involve attributes that are difficult to learn, such as good judgment, good design capabilities and respect for others. At the same time, experience is highly valued, as it defines and supports design direction." Once the first three criteria are evident, a wide range of experience comes into play, including client relations, project management, technical skills, program knowledge, cultural and political savvy, computer modeling and integrated design. In addition to gathering a wide array of talent under one roof, Mithun is also proud of its reputation for mentoring new employees.

MITHUNIVERSITY

Ever since University of Washington professor Omer Mithun founded the firm as a teaching practice in 1949, education has remained a

core value for Mithun and its leadership and it is still a prominent part of strategic planning efforts. Mithun staff members are encouraged to tap out-of-office continuing education opportunities such as AIA classes, University of Washington seminars, and professional certification. Concurrently, "Mithuniversity" offers still more learning venues. Employees and industry professionals alike are invited to broaden staff knowledge through presentations, critique sessions, open debates and discourse.

Mithuniversity offers both required and elective courses in Design, Technical, Project Management and Sustainability. Also woven into the curriculum are regular visits to Mithun job sites, the Distinguished Speaker Series, and Friday lectures – known as "Macademia," an annual visiting professor series that brings outside viewpoints to the firm's thinking and work. Recent speakers have included Jonathan Reich of Cal Poly ("Critical Eco-Literacy"), Raymond Cole of the University of British Columbia ("Building an Environmental Ethic") and Stephen Luoni of the University of Arkansas' Community Design Center, all presenting their latest work and providing a critique of Mithun's new projects. In addition, MIT (Mithun Institute of Technology) programs are lunchtime classes taught by Mithun staff experts on the practical aspects of AutoCAD and other design, word processing and graphic software resources.

Within this rich learning environment, Mithun encourages all interested staff to participate in regular meetings and interactive discussions focused around key areas of the practice, including integrated design, technology, risk management and project management. These lively discussions serve as important mentorship tools for less-experienced designers and often lead to firm-wide

DESIGN AT MITHUN: SEVEN PRINCIPLES

Mithun's "Seven Principles" continue to guide
and inspire its designs across the practice:

Grow an Idea
Expand the Boundaries
Use Nature As a Guide
Create Beauty and Spirit
Do the Math
Strengthen Community
Bring Passion, Leave Ego

SUSTAINABLE PRACTICE: Walking the talk of sustainability is more than a motto within the office – it is a way of worklife: practiced daily and deeply integrated into processes, design philosophy, material choices, commuting, values, and calculation of the staff's collective carbon footprint. Eco board (top) is used in place of foam core for presentations. From coffee grounds to corks, Mithun recycles nearly everything (middle). Reusing tile samples (bottom) from the firm's Materials Library in one of their office kitchens.

"Great projects require great clients, and we work hard to align ourselves with organizations that have congruous missions and visions. One of Mithun's core strengths is that we keep asking questions. Integrated design is not always easy or linear, and team members are continually learning how to improve on working together. Invariably this shared process yields results that exceed expectations. The old model of singular designers dictating an unquestioned design vision does not exist here, and we are better for it."

—Brendan Connolly, AIA, Mithun

initiatives and more formal Mithuniversity courses. Ongoing product lunches with outside vendors are popular as well, covering every conceivable new product or problem-solving technique. Vendors are required to provide educational content during their presentations – in keeping with the culture of continuous learning present in all Mithun-sponsored activities.

Additionally, in-house design critiques are offered every week along Main Street for projects still under development:

> To: All Mithun Users
> Subject: Crit Session #1: First Presbyterian Church of Bellevue - Education Building
>
> Hello All!
> We are re-kicking off the office crits this Thursday, October 26th in Germany at 4pm.
>
> The First Presbyterian Church of Bellevue Team is going to offer up their Education Building project for review and comments. Attached is the event flyer.
>
> Crit Session Goals:
> • Tight budget – how to maximize it
> • Take a look at site systems – how to make it greener, how to make great learning environments and facilitate community
> • Building skin/cladding (esp. materials)
> • How to reduce glazing without negatively impacting daylight, views, or natural ventilation
>
> Please sign-up and participate!

Mithuniversity has twice been recognized by the American Institute of Architects as the best continuing education program in the country, an example of Mithun's academic foundation and continual pursuit of excellence.

STUDY HERE & ABROAD
Another learning opportunity at Mithun occurs with the firm's study trips, a tradition that now dates back more than twenty years. In groups of thirty to thirty-five people, these multi-day trips offer unique insights into the history and architecture of a place, to learn from personal experience how other cultures design, to foster friendships among colleagues. Increasingly, participants find these helpful as well in generating a deeper understanding of urban renewal issues and sustainable design solutions.

The idea for vacation study trips originated with Mithun principal Gerry Cichanski and led to the first trip, to London, in 1986. In addition to touring a number of buildings and construction projects in the city, the Mithun contingent visited architect Richard Rogers' office and the Docklands redevelopment then underway, and later received an incredible behind-the-scenes tour of Lloyds of London. Many more memorable trips would follow, including Paris (1988), Rome (1990), Washington, D.C. (1992), Tokyo/Kyoto (1997), Barcelona (2005) and Buenos Aires (2006). The continued popularity of the program and the firm's steady growth has made it an annual event. As many as one hundred staff members are now eligible to attend these trips, with participants divided into three groups so that a single group travels every year.

THE VIEW FROM HERE: A sketch, a note, the recorded memories of visits to Berlin, Barcelona, New York and Amsterdam – Mithun·sponsored vacation trips present unique opportunities for designers to study the world's best architecture, classic and modern, returning with a changed perspective that inform future design solutions.

INTERNATIONAL SUSTAINABLE SOLUTIONS:
Mithun also participates in an international study tour series
founded on the idea that a common experience and reference point
can cultivate productive dialogue across public agencies, the design
community and private development. To date, several tours have
directly influenced policy and decision-making in the Northwest to
support sustainable community development.

2004, 2005, 2006, 2007, 2008, 2009 · Copenhagen, Denmark/
Malmo, Sweden
Summer 2006 · Berlin, Germany
Spring 2007 · Curitiba, Brazil
Spring 2008 · Shanghai, China
Spring 2009 · Havana, Cuba

MITHUN STUDY TRIPS
1986 · London
1988 · Paris
1990 · Rome
1992 · Washington DC
1994 · Madrid
1997 · Tokyo/Kyoto
1998 · Berlin
2002 · New York / Chicago / Los Angeles
2005 · Barcelona
2006 · Buenos Aires
2007 · Helsinki
2008 · Amsterdam

A CULTURE OF RESEARCH

Research and development has long been ingrained in Mithun's practice – an ongoing pursuit of knowledge to support the evolving science behind sustainability in the built environment. Key areas of interest range from the elimination of invasive plant species to reducing VOC emissions from paints and adhesives to minimizing embodied energy in buildings through alternative and regional building material choices.

Unlike traditional research that takes place within a controlled environment, design innovations at Mithun are tested in the workplace and in real-life settings. In addition to materials research with REI and other clients, Mithun has pursued its own independent work on energy economics, sustainable materials and carbon accounting. Likewise, the firm actively learns from past projects through post occupancy evaluations, undertaken most recently at IslandWood and Epler Hall. By learning how sustainable buildings actually perform relative to initial design goals, designers and planners continually improve upon their green strategies with future projects.

Mithun also initiated breakthrough research in the course of creating its award-winning strategies for Seattle's South Lake Union neighborhood and the Lloyd Crossing District of Portland. Focus areas included carbon sequestration, landscape sequestration, typology, integrated storm water systems, soils and carbon, carbon sequestration materials, and biophilic design. Here, too, questions lead to more questions, research to more research. So collaboration with a growing number of consultants, nonprofits and educators also continues: the Urban Land Institute, the Lady Bird Johnson Wildflower Center, the Cascade Land Conservancy, the Urban Environmental Institute.

IRON DESIGNER! It is a battle of creativity, time, "secret ingredients" – and fun. Inspired by TV's *Iron Chef*, the "Iron Designer" competition annually pits Mithun design teams against each other to fabricate a completely original object, like a steel mesh light fixture.

During each trip, Mithun staff travel together with a developed agenda for study. Knowledge sharing is a key element of the program, so each individual is expected to keep detailed sketches and a journal, then return with slides and present their findings back in the office. In 2007, Brendan Connolly, AIA, captured a dense birch forest just outside Helsinki, using a technique devised to accommodate the bumpy road en route to visiting the Säynatsälo Town Hall during Mithun's study trip to Finland:

> "Visiting at the end of September, our group left rainy Helsinki by bus and reached a birch forest just as the low Nordic sun emerged to illuminate the trees. Our destination was the Säynatsälo Town Hall in Jyväskylä, built in 1952 and designed by Alvar Aalto, the brilliant Finnish architect. Here, as everywhere we have visited so far, we have been impressed with the dynamic quality of light."

Memories like these are added to a published collection of sketches and narratives of places traveled, which is then shared with the rest of the firm. Many trip details and observations find their way into actual design concepts: inspiring ideas for a set of stairs or a green roof – even redefining the public realm of a street to create more park and pedestrian space in the midst of a dense business/retail district.

A COMMUNITY OF COLLABORATORS

Important to building community and camaraderie within the firm, all staff are invited to participate in a number of special activities throughout the year. One of the most anticipated is "Iron Designer," where "designers enter Mithun Stadium and go head to head in the

ultimate design challenge!" For this annual competition modeled after TV's *Iron Chef*, design teams get to demonstrate their ingenuity and collaborative skills. Each team is given a set of pre-determined materials, one "secret ingredient" and forty-five minutes to create and build a special object: maybe a light fixture, maybe a new kind of clock. A panel of judges then critiques all the entries, awarding the title of Iron Designer.

MithunerFest, celebrated each fall, has become one of the firm's four major office parties of the year. Styled after Germany's own Oktoberfest, this special event dates back to 1978 when Fred Brown of Mithun brought the idea with him to the company after living and working in Munich – complete with a rented hall, a keg of beer and lots of German-inspired food. Costumes are highly encouraged. "Bun bowling" remains popular to this day.

Other team and creativity building events include the firm's own distinctive brand of Olympics to coincide with the real worldwide Games, the annual Mithun ArtsFund benefit for arts organizations where employees create art, provide meals and generate experiences to be auctioned, and Mithun cycling teams competing with others in the city to maximize miles ridden during the Cascade Bicycle Club's "Bike to Work Month."

A MATTER OF PROCESS

While expanding and refining its body of work over the past sixty years, Mithun has continued to elevate the quality and rigor of the firm's design processes as well. This approach has also been vital in preserving the core values of the firm and producing great design.

"Urban infill like 200 Occidental is how we're going to adapt our cities over time so they function more like natural ecosystems. They don't have to look natural to function that way. The team kept persevering to figure out how the building could be designed to keep more storm water on site, how to reduce the amount of energy required with a double-skinned system that was also rentable space, and how to fit into the historic scale and context of the neighborhood and park. We needed all the voices at the table to achieve innovation."

—Deb Guenther, ASLA, Mithun

Essential components of this approach include establishing and honoring clear concepts, utilizing strong interdisciplinary teams, and supporting client goals and missions.

Mithun has recognized that the impacts of site and building design reach well beyond property lines. The firm continually endeavors to create design that gives back to the environment and the people who will utilize it. To help implement this thinking over a wide range of projects, the leadership at Mithun defined and implemented "Seven Principles" for design, which serve as both guide and inspiration for project teams and clients. These principles formally reflect attitudes that have always existed at Mithun and focus on the core components of an integrated sustainable design process driven to enhance community, beauty and the environment.

Also supporting designers during the development of projects is the Quality Support team, which includes directors of Integrated Design, Technical Quality and Project Management. A materials resource specialist is committed to researching specified materials and is charged with evaluating the durability, environmental and health impacts of all products specified on projects. Additional contributors to the Mithun process are external discipline experts such as engineers, economists, scientists and contractors. Each expert plays a key role on integrated design teams through his or her collaboration with Mithun designers, urban planners, forest ecologists, graphic designers and cultural auditors in support of clear ideas and effective solutions.

LOOKING INSIDE (WALKING THE TALK)
Mithun applies the same exacting standards internally as its teams

employ on project design and execution. This notion of "walking the talk" is vital to the ongoing success of the firm's practice and culture on numerous levels. Internal processes such as workflow, company policy, quality control, client relations, ethics and sustainability all continue to reflect core values of working creatively, collaboratively, profitably, respectfully, and with integrity.

In 2000, Mithun began to explore The Natural Step (TNS), a process that creates a framework and planning methodology to help organizations build sound sustainable programs within their own offices. A task force was established within the office, charged with having a TNS policy in place by 2004. The next few years were then spent examining ways to define and quantify the firm's carbon footprint beyond the office. Sean Cryan, a sustainability leader at Mithun, noted: "We wanted to look at our impacts on the globe from a social perspective, as well as how much energy we use, where our food is coming from, how we spend our finances, how we compare to other firms in terms of diversity." In turn, this research led to investigating greater use of recycled-content paper, a food waste program, wine cork recycling, the acquisition of a 100 percent hybrid vehicle fleet for the office, and a fleet of office bikes for in-town use.

All of these actions are now integrated into a core firm policy for business practices and projects: reduce energy demand, switch to green power and offset remaining carbon. This philosophy has also resulted in moving to LCD screens for all computers, operating on 100 percent green electrical energy, and becoming the first design firm to join the Chicago Climate Exchange – offsetting its carbon footprint since 2005. Additionally, Mithun provides financial support for employees participating in local utility green power

THE MENTOR: One of many traditions that endure at Mithun is mentoring. Each year on Omer Mithun's birthday – June 10 – a group of five new mentors are selected to coach and share their knowledge with younger designers. And every year since, five more mentors are recognized with a Mithun Mentor stool next to their desks.

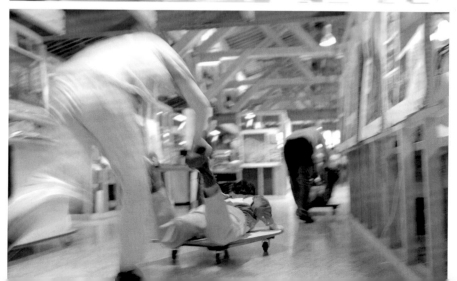

LIFE AND TIMES ON THE PIER: In this open, project-oriented office, it is fitting that Mithun's Model Shop (middle) is located right at the heart of Pier 56: a place for collaboration, where integrated building and landscape designs materialize over the course of days and weeks. Yet having fun is a core value here, too – something Omer Mithun always insisted – by finding ways to blend work and play: like "The Mediocres" (top), a bluesy rock group made up of employees and spouses, or the bi-annual Mithun Olympics (bottom).

42

"Omer instilled in the practice a teaching philosophy, which attracted people who wanted to pursue projects with an academic rigor. This rigor today involves searching for answers through collaborative research to improve the human condition and the planet while merging science and design."

—*Bert Gregory, FAIA, Mithun*

programs and those who elect to use alternative transportation options such as cycling and bus transit to reduce the carbon emissions of their commutes.

MOSS (Mithun Office Sustainability Strategy) has taken this idea one step further. Tied to Mithun's everyday business operations, MOSS supports sustainable initiatives pertaining to process, resources, material and people. Beneath these categories lie tactics to reduce energy (electrical and gas), water and carbon use, and to lessen the firm's production of waste. Initially, the plan relied mostly on individual initiatives: composting, battery recycling, coffee grounds for gardening. Over time, it has led to creation of more and better accounting processes, particularly to track carbon offsets and further quantify the impact of each measure. Meanwhile, MOSS continues to evolve, exploring the use of videoconferencing versus travel and new energy efficiency measures in the office – all informing ideas and design moves that are often shared with clients as well.

BUILDING COMMUNITY
Community – inside and outside of Mithun – means being one of the "100 Best Companies To Work For," numerous speaking engagements, supporting various groups and initiatives with money and pro-bono work, and leadership roles in key civic organizations. It is also volunteering on Habitat for Humanity builds and EarthCorps clean-up days, supporting the Ballard Green Festival, hosting Association of Women Architects (AWA) meetings and the Holiday Auction, and building gingerbread houses and sand castles for charity.

Initiatives that range from participating in national organizations to local and individual efforts engage Mithun on every level as a leader in environmental stewardship. Mithun is a founding member of the Seattle Climate Partnership and the Washington Clean Technology Alliance. Many of the firm's leaders serve on non-profit boards throughout the community, also playing active roles with organizations addressing key regional and national issues that affect the built environment. These organizations include the Association for the Advancement of Sustainability in Higher Education (AASHE), the Governor's Climate Action Team, Puget Sound Regional Council, Cascade Land Conservancy, U.S. Green Building Council, and the Urban Land Institute.

In addition, Mithun has an active, visible role in higher education through sponsorship of the annual Omer Mithun Lecture at the University of Washington's (UW) College of Architecture and Urban Planning. The firm's recent endowment of the Mithun/Russell Family Foundation Professorship at UW is designed to help bridge many of the divisions typically found between departments at universities and encourage sustainable, interdisciplinary thinking and collaboration. The first individuals named to the professorship were Steve Kieran, FAIA and James Timberlake, FAIA of KieranTimberlake Associates.

For its design leadership and firm-wide commitment to "walking the talk" on environmental strategies, Mithun was given a USGBC Local/Regional Leadership award in 2004. Further acknowledgement of Mithun's sustainability practices and internal processes came in June 2008 when it was honored as the "Greenest of the Green" company in the state by Washington CEO Magazine, which declared, "This is a company that goes a step beyond, a company that gets it".[1]

MITHUN CLIMATE PARTNERSHIP

In January 2007, the Mithun Climate Partnership was launched to promote personal reductions in energy demand, along with purchases of green power and carbon offsets. Mithun has committed to share with staff, on a 50-50 basis, the cost of the following Personal Climate Protection Actions:

- Reduce Demand: Mithun will match any recognized utility energy incentive program for a Mithun staff member's primary residence for the following items: installation of building insulation, hot water heaters, washer and dryer, and permanently-installed lighting and heating equipment.

- Switch to Green Power: Mithun will share 50 percent of the cost to any Mithun staff for enrolling in a recognized utility green power program for a primary residence.

- Offset Remaining Carbon: Mithun will share 50 percent of the cost to Mithun staff electing to offset their family's carbon footprint through the Climate Trust's carbon offset program.

DOWN MAIN STREET: Oversized displays highlighting the diverse nature of work at Mithun – interiors, architecture, landscape architecture and urban planning concepts – line "Main Street", the central walkway running through its Pier 56 office on the waterfront.

PRINCIPLE 2

EXPAND THE BOUNDARIES

THE BLUE RING STRATEGY

"Thirty-eight percent of Seattle's city center is in the public realm. It's huge. We can use it any way we want. The Blue Ring Strategy teaches us to look at everything we own in common: the streets, the sidewalks, the parks, all of it outside of property lines. We wanted to understand things, to figure out a way to improve this interface between private and public, the challenge of this new century."

—*Bert Gregory, FAIA, Mithun*

THE BLUE RING STRATEGY
Seattle, Washington

June 2002

"Creating a lively, sustainable, connected public realm"

Named for the "blue ring" of water and rain that geographically defines Seattle, it is the most significant long-range master plan for the city in more than a century. The Blue Ring Strategy, for the City of Seattle, is designed to create a new framework of urban open spaces and connections and result in more livable neighborhoods within the central part of the city.

Mithun led development of "Seattle's Open Space Strategy for the Center City", inspired by the Olmsted Brothers' "Green Ring" network of parks and parkways. But unlike that plan of 1903, open spaces in Seattle's evolving downtown today are scattered and not well-defined. A Blue Ring system would link waterfront and urban parks as well as civic and cultural destinations like Seattle Center and Pike Place Market with pedestrian-friendly streets. This 100-year vision, which received ASLA's 2003 Honor Award for Analysis and Planning, begins with a series of policy changes, incentives, partnerships, and guidelines for open space development over the next decade. The dream of the Blue Ring may be realized someday soon: full of spaces for social gatherings and recreation, connecting Seattle citizens with the water's edge at Lake Union and Elliott Bay, places to inspire, places to enjoy the urban lifestyle of the Northwest.

INTEGRATED DESIGN: MITHUN

Going beyond. It is a quality prized at Mithun – and encouraged among clients, collaborators, even end users of the buildings and places they create. Expand the boundaries has no beginning and no end, it just is: a way of being, the pursuit of an ideal, moving beyond ordinary, embracing sustainability in new and often unexpected ways. For one new community, It means letting a salmon-bearing stream respect no boundaries, to function as nature intended. It is a gymnasium designed to maximize natural daylight. Or a 100-year master plan to build great cities by preserving forests, farmland and other open spaces and, as a consequence, drive local economies.

The best projects question everything. Is your goal to build a building? Or does it represent a broader question about place and community that should be answered?

Curiosity, inquisitiveness: how to bring habitat and vegetation back into urban places – mixing green and gray in a city environment. Redefining the use of space. Understanding the past to imagine the future.

The boundaries may be physical – or they may be dictated by ownership and politics. Overcoming those barriers begins by asking "What if?" By understanding the natural edges of a project. By communicating change over time. By asking what if we did not always have to turn on the lights in a room? Or could a neighborhood function naturally as it did before there even was a neighborhood? Coaxing, questioning, pushing the limits – Mithun's designers work to redefine codes and policy, to integrate art and science, to reweave the civic fabric through private/public partnerships that achieve a new level of sustainable design.

CHAPTER 3:
A FUTURE THAT DEFINES US

"As we look to the future, we need to move forward in a very integrated fashion to ensure that our cities are as healthy and restorative as we can make them. Our goal at Mithun is to contribute to that effort, to pursue more scientific inquiry, more research on materials, systems, skins and products associated with buildings – to move beyond traditional architecture, planning, landscape architecture and interior design work. We are at a time, an incredibly exciting time, when we strive to create designs that are as elegant as a flower."

—Bert Gregory, FAIA, Mithun

GREEN RESORT: Mithun's designs for the Miraval Life in Balance Resort and Spa near Tucson include rammed earth walls made from desert soil and cement – while the décor of new sustainable guest rooms reflects the earth tones and natural materials found in the surrounding landscape.

SEEKING, FINDING, UNDERSTANDING, EXPLORING FURTHER, MAPPING A NEW PATH TO SUSTAINABILITY

"It is not the answers that show us the way, but the questions."
Rainer Maria Rilke

If, as Shakespeare wrote, "What is past is prologue", then Mithun's future is assured to be one of innovation, integrated design, and creating places that celebrate natural systems and spaces for people that encourage community. It is certain to focus on cities and smart growth, on higher density development, on a deeper understanding of the urban ecosystem. Design in the 21st century for Mithun will continue to pay special attention to the needs of young and old: to learning environments for children as well as respectful, affordable housing for seniors and low income populations. It will also increasingly explore the impacts of climate change, land use issues and urban agriculture, new transit possibilities, the critical importance of watersheds, and restorative design for streetscapes, urban shorelines, wetlands, forests, historic structures and neighborhoods.

Just as Mithun's breakthrough designs at REI Seattle, REI Denver and IslandWood led to the living building concepts of the Center for Urban Agriculture, so, too, the creation of Seattle's Blue Ring Strategy and the South Lake Union "Resource Guide" made possible the Lloyd Crossing Urban Design Plan as a sustainable blueprint for cities in the years ahead. Mithun looks beyond green buildings, beyond neighborhood planning, to the larger design questions of whole cities and regions in coming decades. In 2007, the firm developed a web-based tool, BuildCarbonNeutral.org, for calculating and reducing greenhouse gas emissions during building and site construction. Its co-sponsorship and ongoing support of Seattle's 2008 ULI Reality Check could mean a significant new direction for housing, transportation, land preservation and green building practices for the Puget Sound region. And as a Cascade Land Conservancy partner, Mithun's contributions to the 100-year Cascade Agenda support a new model for conservation across the nation that is built on the interdependence of urban and rural quality.

For Mithun, the seeds of its future emerged long ago as the organization's collaborative spirit, the pursuit of a true multidisciplinary approach to design – driving complex responses to increasingly complex issues while creating the elements of a built environment never attempted before. Ultimately, there is a fundamental truth here, one shared organizational trait that drives and inspires Mithun in its work: the courage to question.

BUILDING A NEW NORTHWEST

Mithun continues to build on its successes over the last few years with a series of progressive design and planning commissions. Each in its own way is helping to create a shift, a new model for sustainable design: in urban infill, affordable housing, the economics of ecological systems, site specific green infrastructure, low impact development, buildings that teach, and clean technology incubators.

Like West Seattle's High Point Community, New Columbia (2007) in Portland revitalizes a distressed public housing site into a vibrant, mixed-income community. Mithun collaborated with the Housing Authority of Portland to explore the boundaries of smart growth: high-density, sustainability, security and accessibility. As with High Point, this redeveloped neighborhood has been reintegrated into the pattern of streets and homes that surrounds it. New amenities include parks, community college classrooms, a school, and retail destinations. But in addition to an extensive "green street" system of vegetated pocket swales, what makes New Columbia special is that approximately 98 percent of all stormwater stays on site, using an innovative collection and treatment scheme to further reduce impacts to the Columbia River Slough.

In the heart of Seattle's historic Pioneer Square, 200 Occidental promises to create a 21st century expression within a revitalizing downtown environment. When complete, this ten-story mixed-use development will feature flexible office space over ground-floor retail, residential apartments, an internal above-grade parking system, and a rooftop gathering space for the community, connecting people with views to Puget Sound and the Olympic Mountains. Mithun's design targets LEED® Platinum, incorporating materials and proportions that respect the neighborhood's existing architecture, while a high-performance curtain wall provides solar screening, sun shading and a reflective backdrop to Occidental Park – Pioneer Square's historic public park and fine grain of streets and alleys.

Kitsap SEED, southwest of Seattle, is laying the groundwork for a visionary design that will provide new water, habitat and energy resources on the site of a former naval dumping ground. With construction underway in fall 2008, this new business park for clean energy technology companies will showcase the highest level of sustainable development and business operating practices. Here, Mithun aims to meet 2030 Challenge targets with LEED® Platinum buildings and site design: net zero energy, carbon neutral, native plant community restoration, and a soil system that turns the entire property into a "stormwater facility", allowing for 100 percent bioretention of rainwater.

Near Woodinville, Washington is Brightwater – slated to be the most modern wastewater treatment plant in the nation when it opens in 2010. The facility will feature state-of-the-art systems for wastewater, odor control, reclaimed water, and quality of effluent discharged into Puget Sound. But that is only part of the design story. The new

DEEP STUDY: Whether materials testing or post-occupancy evaluation, research remains an essential part of the practice: to "question everything" while furthering the art and science of sustainability. For the Kitsap SEED project for the Port of Bremerton, designers created a matrix (top) comparing the efficacy of different plant systems. The Seattle University Sustainable Master Plan examined carbon sequestration by soil type (middle). And a partnership with the Lady Bird Johnson Wildflower Center yielded the BuildCarbonNeutral online calculator (bottom). [1]

53

200 OCCIDENTAL: Renewal with a sustainable gesture to the future – that is the theme behind Mithun's design of 200 Occidental, a mixed-use urban infill in the historic Pioneer Square neighborhood of Seattle. The site of parking lot for the past forty years, this ten-story development, for Urban Visions, includes 126,000 square feet of loft-style office space over ground-floor retail and 50,000 square feet of residential apartments facing Occidental Park.

1 metric tonne CO₂

THE CARBON EQUATION: In promoting renewable energy, carbon offsets and other design and corporate strategies to reduce greenhouse gas emissions, a Mithun presentation may include creative examples that illustrate 1 metric tonne of carbon dioxide: a cube 33 feet to a side. The average American is responsible for 24 metric tonnes of CO_2-equivalent emissions per year.

Brightwater Treatment Plant covers one hundred-ten acres, most of it on greyfield and brownfield sites. One-third of this area will be devoted to wastewater operations. Mithun is working collaboratively with Hargreaves Associates, the lead landscape architects, to create a public park-like setting for another third – to include stormwater detention ponds and marshes, pathways, boardwalks and extensive native landscaping. The remaining third will be restored as natural Pacific Northwest habitat. Water also informed the design process for Brightwater's Environmental Education and Community Center: stormwater runoff from the treatment plant roofs and hardscape is collected and treated on-site in a series of detention ponds that become part of the overall landscape. The building's form itself creates a marriage between the environment, the site and functional spaces – designed to capture light, improve cross ventilation, shed water, and control sun and rain exposure.

FURTHER EXPLORATIONS
While the majority of Mithun projects over the past six decades have been located west of the Rockies – and particularly Washington State, Oregon and Northern California – it was only a matter of time before the firm's national reputation for sustainable design would bring its architects, urban planners, landscape architects and interior designers to the Southwest, the Gulf Coast and elsewhere.

There has never seemed to be a compelling enough reason to consider an additional office outside Seattle. Until now. Mithun's leadership has insisted the firm's focus remain squarely on quality, not quantity, while retaining the values of its unique corporate culture. Yet recently the people, place and projects all aligned to

support the idea of a Mithun presence in San Francisco. From its new office at Market and Montgomery downtown, Mithun will have a solid base in the midst of the city's dynamic green building market to continue its work along the West Coast and on an increasing number of Bay Area residential, commercial and institutional projects.

The hospitality market has long been a fixture of the practice. So the opportunity to influence the sustainable design of a new eco resort made perfect sense. Mithun has led redevelopment of the award-winning Miraval Life in Balance Resort and Spa near Tucson since 2007, beginning with a master plan to align the resort's physical environment with its spa experience. Phased projects include renovation of Miraval's signature spa and fitness center, as well as new buildings for wellness, meditation, yoga, outdoor treatments and new sustainable guest rooms.

Mithun's work on the new Nordic Heritage Museum in Seattle will expand the facility into a contemporary cultural center that reaches a wider audience. In addition to regular exhibit space, the new museum will feature performance spaces and classrooms, supporting the Scandinavian Language Institute, woodcarving classes and painting. The Southeastern U.S., too, has been unexplored territory for Mithun. In June 2008, the firm was commissioned to design the new Early Learning Village for the Louisiana Children's Museum in New Orleans. Reopening ten months after Hurricane Katrina had devastated the city, it was clear the museum's role had to adapt to meet the changing realities of families in a rebuilding community. Evolving into a parent resource center and a healing place for children to connect with nature, the museum will be relocated from the historic Warehouse District downtown to a twelve acre site in New Orleans'

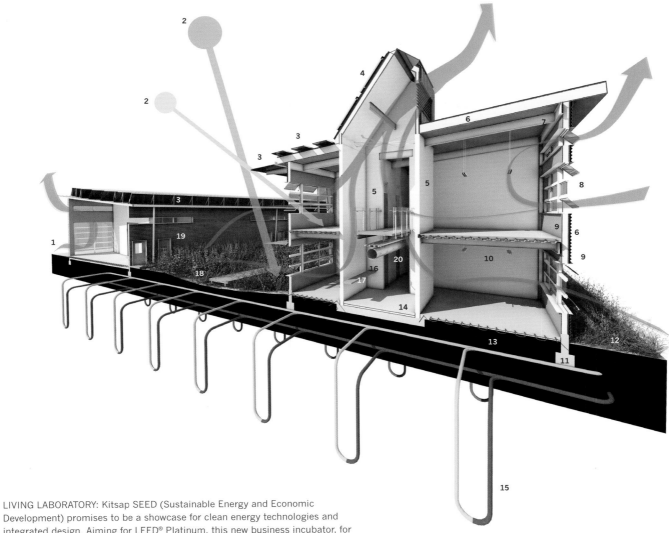

LIVING LABORATORY: Kitsap SEED (Sustainable Energy and Economic Development) promises to be a showcase for clean energy technologies and integrated design. Aiming for LEED® Platinum, this new business incubator, for the Port of Bremerton, near Seattle draws upon the broadest array of design and planning disciplines at Mithun yet.

1 porous concrete to maximize site stormwater infiltration
2 optimized building orientation for active and passive solar capture
3 143 kw photovoltaic panel array
4 solar thermal collectors (22 kw energy contribution)
5 masonry shear cores provide daylighting, high thermal mass and stack-aided natural cooling (fan assist)
6 structural insulated panel system
7 modular structural steel frame to enhance building flexibility for changing user needs
8 operable windows provide natural cooling and daylight harvesting
9 high recycled content, low voc and regionally produced materials
10 high efficiency l.e.d. and fluorescent interior and exterior lighting

11 high fly ash content structural concrete
12 reclamation of former naval dumping facility site
13 radiant in-floor heating and free cooling
14 social gathering nodes encourage interaction and creative exchange of ideas geothermal heat exchangers
15 expressed building systems to enhance user awareness and connection to
16 resource use
17 fsc certified regional wood products
18 bioretention area collects excess roof stormwater to achieve 65/10/0 low impact site stormwater strategy
19 site stormwater collection and re-use
20 heat recovery ventilation

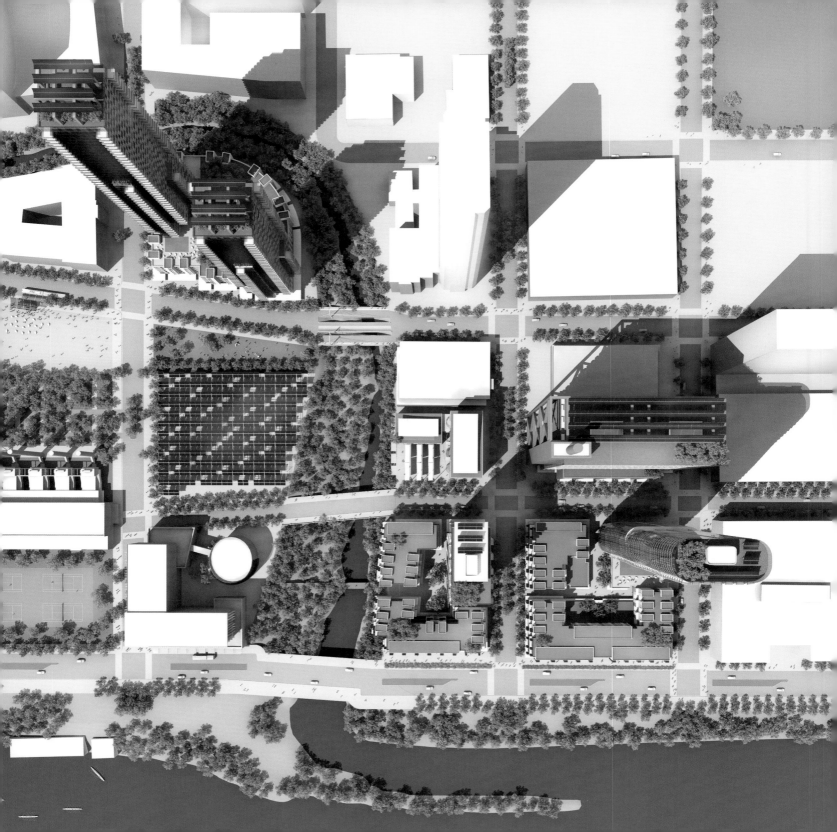

URBAN CORE: Dubbed "Project Green", the nearly seven acre redevelopment for downtown Austin will be the largest the city has ever seen – featuring five towers with green roofs and a field of PV arrays to generate clean energy. Mithun's master plan for this project (with Trammel Crow Company, Constructive Ventures Inc., and USAA Real Estate), on the site of a decommissioned water treatment plant, creates a sustainable district of offices, hotels, retail and residential spaces plus a network of pedestrian alleys, bike trails and civic courtyards.

City Park. Sustainability and stewardship are overarching themes. Through Mithun's collaborative planning process, the Village will offer interactive experiences indoors and outdoors. The museum hopes to serve as a national model of the living building and learning environment, with the first phase open by 2010.

NEAR AND FAR, THE MASTER PLAN
In its Lloyd Crossing Plan for the City of Portland, Mithun effectively establishes a thirty-five block inner-city neighborhood that mimics the carbon footprint and natural systems of a pristine forest. Looking ahead, Bert Gregory and others at Mithun see the 2004 plan as the center of a sustainability "ripple" moving outward to other neighborhoods and other cities, as new master planning commissions for the firm represent several opportunities for "Lloyd Crossing realized".

"Lloyd Crossing needs to happen everywhere," says Gregory. "As Portland builds upon its journey for the next fifty years, the elements and lessons of Lloyd will be helpful as the city moves forward to an integrated infrastructure, district water and energy strategies, demand reduction, and carbon-neutral neighborhoods. Lloyd is certainly one vision of the future of cities."

Downtown Austin, Texas may become another of those ripples. The city's "Project Green" aims for a 22nd century approach to open space, economic development, affordable housing, and low-impact design. The Mithun-led master plan will transform five city blocks in the footprint of a decommissioned water treatment plant into a vibrant, transit-oriented urban neighborhood. This development

will include 2.6 million square feet of office, hotel, residential, retail and parking space, as well as an extensive public realm of streets, pedestrian alleys, bike trails, civic plazas and courtyards. Developers are seeking LEED® Gold certification for the entire project, its buildings outfitted with solar thermal collectors, double skin membranes, solar screens, water reuse systems, and vegetated roofs. In addition, Project Green is designed to eliminate potable water use and to achieve carbon neutral operations through energy efficiency, onsite and offsite renewable power, and utilization of the city's district cooling system. Mithun's design would augment urban food production and a popular community agriculture program. And finally, the interconnection of pedestrian, transit and bike routes will link a series of flexible outdoor spaces and create new venues for the city's thriving music scene.

The scope of Mithun's sustainable planning expertise continues to grow and expand, particularly as the firm taps new opportunities in higher education and healthcare across the country. At Pacific Lutheran University (Tacoma), Seattle University, South Seattle Community College and the University of Virginia (Richmond), master planning efforts include Lloyd Crossing-style analyses to push the boundaries for incorporating sustainable strategies on campus.

Along Tulalip Bay, up the coast from Seattle, Mithun's award-winning work for the Tulalip Tribes of Washington highlights the firm's use of participatory processes and careful technical and cultural analyses. With the population of the tribe expected to double over the next decade, tribal leaders recognized the need to plan for the future. Mithun's master plan for a new administration building and gathering hall successfully brings over seventy office locations across

These diagrams show the Blue Ring Strategies in action · repairing the urban fabric with new streetscape designs and phased mixed-use development moving from (left to right) plaza to street to neighborhood

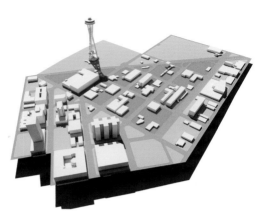 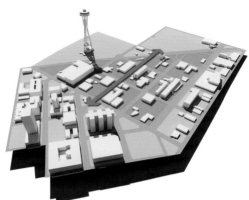 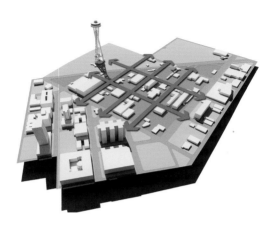

TAYLOR 28:
"Greening the urban right-of-way"

In the shadow of the Space Needle, not far from Seattle's equally famous Monorail, lies a forgotten place, an undefined neighborhood of large, mostly one-story warehouses and commercial spaces. The near-freeway scale of Taylor Avenue between Denny Way and John Street is dominated by concrete and the adjacent asphalt parking lots. But that scene is rapidly changing with Taylor 28: a radical new streetscape design and residential, mixed-used development for BRE Properties Development Inc., led by Mithun.

A key element of the Blue Ring Strategy, the project is also tied to Seattle's Street Edge Alternatives program, designed to bring nature back into the public realm. First, a large part (eighteen feet) of Taylor Avenue – underused, for angled parking – will be transformed into a plaza street; this design allows for a wide pedestrian zone

(thirty-eight feet) along the eastern edge. A planting strip and colonnade trees at the curb buffer pedestrians from the street, the plaza area interspersed with raingardens and movable and built-in seating to create a series of "outdoor rooms". Through the use of native plants and permeable paving, the entire plaza is designed to capture 28,000 gallons of stormwater – achieving zero discharge during a 25-year storm. Ultimately, Mithun's plan re-imagines Seattle streets as a new kind of open space to enhance community within the urban core.

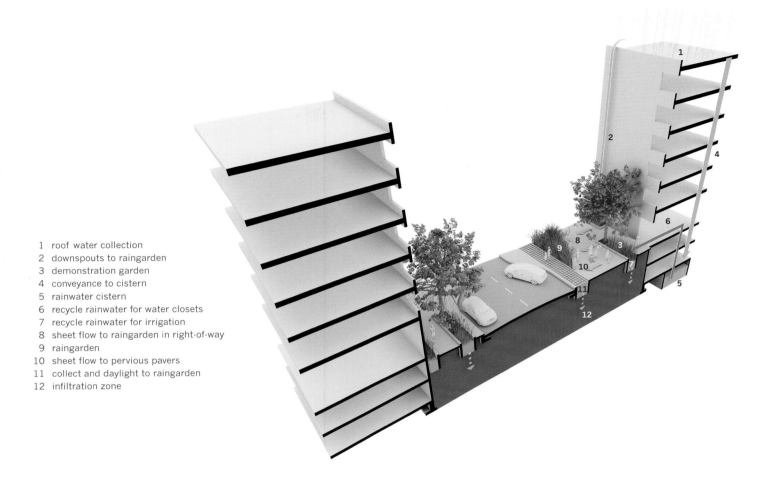

1 roof water collection
2 downspouts to raingarden
3 demonstration garden
4 conveyance to cistern
5 rainwater cistern
6 recycle rainwater for water closets
7 recycle rainwater for irrigation
8 sheet flow to raingarden in right-of-way
9 raingarden
10 sheet flow to pervious pavers
11 collect and daylight to raingarden
12 infiltration zone

Taylor 28, Seattle, Washington

Spring 2009

Mixed use development/streetscape, 160,000 square feet, 1.2 acre site

Rain gardens, permeable and specialty pavement, native plantings, roof water collection, material deconstruction and reuse.

"Taylor 28 lies within this unclaimed urban triangle, a 'no man's land' of pavement and parking spaces surrounded by four different neighborhoods. There is an opportunity here for us to create experiences for people, to demonstrate a better use of open space connections – from water to water and park to park – as part of Seattle's Blue Ring Strategy."

—T. Frick, ASLA, Mithun

TRIBES OF TULALIP: As the spiritual and economic center of the reservation, Tulalip Bay also becomes the focal point in creating a fully sustainable community over the next decade for the Tulalip Tribes, a group of Native American peoples living in Washington's mid-Puget Sound region. The award-winning Tulalip Bay Vision Plan and Tulalip Bay Reservation Master Plan by Mithun also led to development of a new 75,000-square-foot administration building for the tribe.

"The development [Project Green] is a keystone site for downtown Austin along Second Street. The neighborhood's pedestrian scale knits together the fabric of several downtown areas through better public transportation, pedestrian, and bicycle access, and provides a great range of different uses that complement each other. It is a wonderful opportunity to connect people to nature through improvements to Shoal Creek and linked public spaces."

—Deb Guenther, ASLA, Mithun

the reservation under one roof and provides a place for fifteen hundred tribal members to meet for dinners and celebrations. Out of this, too, was born a strategy to protect and restore the important spiritual, natural and community components of Tulalip Bay and the reservation. Both the Tulalip Bay Vision Plan and the Tulalip Bay Reservation Master Plan exemplify how Mithun was able to weave together the multiple voices of science, native cultures and design. Here, they have demonstrated it is possible to provide for housing growth, recover the water's edge, restore the bay as the heart of the Tulalip Tribes, and redevelop the community's green infrastructure by 2020 – and beyond.

Seeking, testing, exploring new concepts for a new era: it has always been the way of Mithun's designers –looking to push the boundaries of LEED®, to realize living buildings, restored environments, and vibrant, high performing places for people. Now, at 60, Mithun sets its sights on the future: rebuilding and re-envisioning urban infrastructure; achieving zero energy, carbon and water neutrality and other new benchmarks in integrated design; and participating in the policy-making of a region through active involvement in the Seattle Climate Partnership, the Puget Sound Regional Council, the Cascadia Region Green Building Council and others.

Indeed, at Mithun this is a time for promise, to glimpse ahead, just the beginning of what is yet to come.

CHAPTER 4:
DESIGNING THE REI EXPERIENCE

INTRODUCTION

DESIGNING THE REI EXPERIENCE
Seattle & Denver Flagship Stores

"If you aren't living on the edge, you are taking up too much space."
Jim Whittaker, first American to summit Mount Everest and former CEO of REI

"REI was located in a wonderful old building with a maze of spaces up-and-down that was quite fascinating. They needed more room and a modern store to redefine their retail operations. As is often the case, the architectural process is one vehicle to help a company evolve to the next level. And so we embarked on a journey together that would extend to more than thirty locations."

—*Bert Gregory, FAIA, Mithun*

It all began with a Swiss ice ax – which bore an idea, an innovation, an image that would later become an architectural icon in retailing. Started in 1938 by a group of Pacific Northwest climbers, Recreational Equipment, Inc. (REI), has become the nation's largest consumer cooperative, specializing in outdoor adventure gear and clothing for hiking, climbing, camping, bicycling, paddling and winter sports.

In that same tradition, Mithun's design of the REI Seattle and Denver flagship stores effectively transformed two urban neighborhoods, changed the face of merchandising and launched sustainable principles into the mainstream.

REI SEATTLE FLAGSHIP

Seattle, Washington

All of Seattle was surprised in the early 1990s when the member-owned cooperative decided to move its famous flagship store from the city's Capitol Hill neighborhood to a new location near Seattle's city center. The well-loved old store had grown in "helter-skelter fashion" over decades to occupy five levels and multiple buildings along Pike Street.

Yet, at nearly 100,000 square feet, the store's Grand Opening on September 13, 1996 marked a fresh start for the co-op. Mithun's striking design of the new flagship captures the spirit of a Cascade mountain lodge with heavy timber trusses and "forest-like" volumes of space. "We wanted to create an urban building reflecting the concepts of those types of structures in an architecturally appropriate, modern way," said Bert Gregory.

Mountains, streams, boulders, daylight, native Pacific Northwest forest – a patch of paradise just minutes from the heart of Seattle. These natural elements, representing the conservation values of its members and carefully crafted into the design of the store, instantly turned REI Seattle into a top tourist spot.

DESIGN OVERVIEW

The Seattle flagship and environs have been referred to as the making of a "place" that contributes to the identity of a region. It is a place featuring natural light, wood, stone and an emphasis on structure, connections and concern for the environment through the building's resource-efficient form and construction techniques.

Fundamentally, the architecture reflects the alley and grid pattern of a Cascade neighborhood: the large front porch capturing daylight as the sun moves from east to west. Further reinforcing that regional identity is a northwest landscape created especially for visitors to the store. This outdoor urban courtyard is a forest of spruce and fir trees surrounding a thirty-foot-high waterfall that cascades over a series of boulders to a pond below.

To Bus Stop

CONSERVATION ETHIC: The REI site design reflects the co-op's enduring commitment to outdoor recreation, responding to climate while immersing customers in nature as they enter the store.

1 elevator/stair tower to parking
2 entry porch
3 gear test, hiking/biking trails
4 sub-alpine forest
5 climbing pinnacle

TRANSFORMED SPACE: What was once a commercial/warehouse district adjacent to the busy I-5 Expressway north of downtown Seattle became a 1.2-acre neighborhood park – a carefully-crafted slice of the Cascades embracing the store's façade and main entrance.

"This REI is the flagship of 46 stores nationwide. This REI has 1.4 million active members. This store doesn't have that same musty, creosote smell of the old Capitol Hill flagship store it's replacing.

But in other ways, this is the same REI the Andersons founded."

—*Knight Ridder/Tribune Business News 09/11/1996*

INTEGRATED DESIGN PROCESS

Mithun designers sat down with REI's owner/senior management group and the general contractor to establish the vision and objectives for the project in a crucial all-day goal-setting session. The outcome: REI wanted a green building within cost constraints and without compromising co-op member dividends.

Through a collaborative planning process, they further identified several action items:
- Transform and catalyze an urban neighborhood
- Challenge traditional codes and construction
- Launch sustainability as a global brand
- Reintroduce natural habitat to a warehouse district
- Create an experiential retail setting
- Achieve an enduring legacy

A survey of REI's membership and employees offered additional high-level goals and criteria. They wanted the building to reflect the company's commitment to the environment. They wanted it to be authentic: it had to feel good and fit "like an old shoe" (an homage to the old store). And it needed to convey a strong sense of service and heritage, reflect a clubhouse atmosphere, and provide interactive opportunities. Under Mithun's direction, the architecture, interior design, landscape architecture and engineering concepts were all carefully meshed with REI's conservation values, mission and drive to innovate.

THE SITE

The new site chosen for the flagship store was essentially a "no man's land" of warehouses and commercial buildings located only a block from Interstate 5. After conducting urban design studies of the neighborhood, Mithun proposed a change in the street grid so that the building could serve as a buffer between the freeway and a simulated forest planned for the southwest corner of the lot.

Working closely with the Berger Partnership, the project's landscape architects, the team devised a "decompression landscape" for visitors to pass through before entering the store. The result: a forest rich in sixty different plant species native to Northwest woodlands, next to fallen cedar logs and boulders and with views of a pond and waterfall. Approximately twenty-one thousand square feet of the 1.2-acre site was set aside for this courtyard, crisscrossed by hiking paths and a 470-foot outdoor mountain-bike test trail for customers. The constructed waterfall is fed by recirculated rainwater from the store's roof and serves an additional purpose by generating white noise to mask the sound of freeway traffic nearby.

THE PROGRAM

The store's many new features quickly made it a destination for tourists visiting Seattle and the Pacific Northwest. Chief among these is the REI Pinnacle, the tallest free-standing indoor climbing structure in the world – a recognized landmark along I-5, especially when lit up at night.

The 110-ton, sixty-five-foot-high rock – set inside a glass enclosure – can accommodate as many as fifteen climbers at a time, and from the top offers great views of Puget Sound and the Olympic Mountains. Due to zoning restrictions that limit the footprint of an enclosure this high to sixteen hundred square feet, Mithun's designers placed the

framing structure outside rather than inside the glass. This design feature made it possible for the rock to remain indoors and comply with codes. The height of the tower also aids in ventilation of the entire retail space, moving hot air up and out of the store.

Climbing is REI's legacy. So, at the store's main entrance there are heavy wooden doors featuring ice axes for handles. Immediately inside is a space devoted to the REI story: museum-quality displays that tell the rich heritage of the co-op dating back nearly seventy years, of the founders Lloyd and Mary Anderson, of 1963's American Mount Everest Expedition with Jim Whittaker, later to become the company's CEO, and more.

Flexibility, navigation and interaction are the keys to the program. Because the store's structure is largely exposed, the city would not permit it to function as one building. Instead, Mithun divided retail areas between two distinct, connected buildings. The main retail space is open, with five "specialty shops" spread over two levels and connected by two main sets of semi-circular staircases. The location of each shop may change according to season, sales or display requirements. In addition to merchandise, these shops service gear and feature interactive user areas. A "rain room" showers water on customers who try out waterproof clothing. There are camp-stove-testing and water-filter-testing areas next to the store's campsite and stream.

Rounding out the program upstairs is a bicycle shop, a small café and several meeting rooms free to area non-profits – adding to the store's popularity as a public space in Seattle and contributing a sense of community to this warehouse district.

STRUCTURE & MATERIALS

The structural design of the store is practical, functional, without any extraneous details – just like REI's own climbing gear.

Mithun designed the flagship's systems – every bolt, every gusset, every tie rod – to express the honesty of all the connections. This system is a variation of the super-efficient "Berkeley System", like those used to build warehouses. In addition, the giant beams overhead are comprised of smaller glue-lam Douglas Fir pieces so that less wood was needed and board members are structurally more efficient. The use of two-by-fours every two feet on center, then running the glue-lams every eight feet on center up to the roof, provides important retail clear space and allows interior store layout to remain flexible.

The prominent use of salvaged wood, unpainted steel and other materials still in a raw state reflect REI's preference for authenticity. The exterior features concrete retaining walls, gray corrugated metal wall panels for the cladding, and glue-lam Douglas Fir for the columns and supports over the store's porch and entrance. Many interior details and materials are purposely rough as well. These materials include reclaimed Douglas Fir timbers suspended from the ceiling. Steel-frame windows were salvaged from old buildings previously on the site. Reminiscent of the old store are suspended metal halide lamps, exposed galvanized ductwork, and even brick flooring brought over from REI's former location.

To reduce the upkeep of paints and finishes, the store's interior walls are lined with a modular system of cedar veneer panels over plywood. Together with the concrete and steel (allowed to rust), the

SPACIOUS, COMFORTABLE, HONEST: Materials selected for the building interior have since become signature elements of REI's store design: rough-hewn wood, unfinished steel, concrete, stone and galvanized metal throughout – raw, natural and authentic.

color and palette of this wood provides a natural backdrop for the outdoor clothing and gear on display. Additionally, 4 X 8 sheets of OSB wallboard (an inexpensive, engineered wood product), stained in natural shades of green or yellow, serve to distinguish different specialty shops from each other on both levels of the store.

ENERGY

REI-Seattle features an array of energy-saving strategies, from solar orientation to a computer-controlled energy management system to carbon monoxide sensors that activate exhaust fans in the 475-car underground garage.

HEATING & COOLING

Redefining the parameters of comfort and convincing the client to include unconditioned spaces turned out to be key design moves. With a base comfort zone of 70 degrees F, REI agreed to temperature swings of up to 5 degrees in certain areas. In turn, this decision enabled the co-op to downsize equipment, invest less capital in the beginning, and ultimately, lower operating costs.

This temperature variation is most evident within the store's signature Climbing Wall enclosure. At the top, temperatures can reach the 90s F in summer, a condition not acceptable to most retailers. This portion of the building uses air from the retail area to partially temper the space as computerized louvers bring in outside air to create a stack effect.

In addition, the new building was sited to optimize solar energy

collection. Morning light helps to warm the space before the store opens at 9 A.M., while the large louvers protect southern and western façades to minimize heat build-up.

LIGHTING & DAYLIGHTING

From morning's eastern light until the sun sets, REI-Seattle relies heavily on daylighting – quite unusual for a retail environment at the time it first opened. This feature provides a crucial connection to the outdoors and, as Gregory phrases it, "a portal to nature."

REI saw an immediate benefit to customers through prominent use of daylight and windows. REI was willing to forego standard lighting schemes and give up prime wall space that would normally have been filled with merchandise displays. High-efficiency metal halide fixtures supplement the extensive daylighting, with some fluorescent track lighting to highlight special areas. Also, motion lighting sensors detect occupancy after hours, and high-efficiency sodium vapor lighting is used in garages.

THE FOREST: Visitors make their way through native firs and cedars and past a thirty-foot-high waterfall before reaching the store's 'front porch'. This constructed landscape serves a dual purpose: masking the noise of heavy traffic on the freeway nearby and creating a transition space for customers, from city street to mountain retreat.

REI STORY: Immediately inside, Seattle's entrance sequence narrates the rich heritage of REI, how the Co-op was founded in 1938 by a group of climbing enthusiasts and the first American expedition to Mt. Everest.

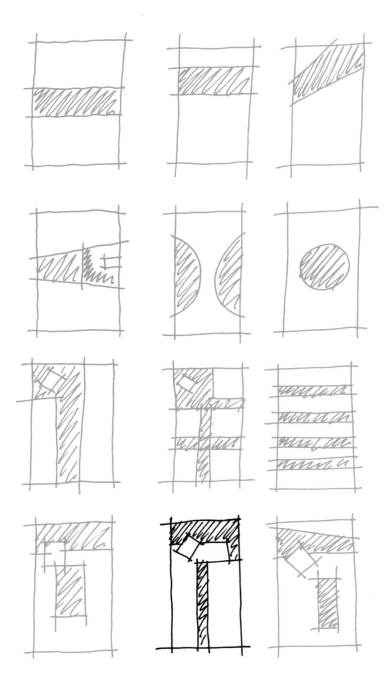

ECO DESIGN/BREAKTHROUGH RETAILING:
Mithun's 1993 concept sketches for a
new REI·Seattle Flagship store reflect a
completely new kind of retail environment
and its response to climate, sun angles, air
and natural light.

NATURAL COOLING: The store's innovative design relies on fresh air minimizing mechanical ventilation in portions of the building · the cool courtyard air moves into the unconditioned REI Story space, then up and out through the Climbing Wall enclosure in a thermal stack effect. The courtyard also provides the fresh air for the parking garage.

1 gear test, hiking/biking trails, sub-alpine forest
2 cafe
3 elevator/stair tower to parking
4 porch
5 climbing pinnacle
6 pinnacle and entry area conditioned by air exhausted from building
7 garage ventilated with fresh air from west

THE REI STORY

1938: A group of climbers led by Lloyd Anderson forms
      Recreational Equipment, Inc. (REI)
1944: REI opens its first retail location
1996: The new Seattle flagship store opens, named Top Ten
      Green [1998]
1997: REI Bloomington (Minneapolis area) opens
2000: REI opens its first international store, in suburban
      Tokyo
2000: A second REI flagship store opens in Denver, later
      named Top Ten Green [2001]
2004: REI's Portland, Oregon store is the first retail store in
      the country to earn LEED-CI® Gold
2006: REI's Pittsburgh store earns LEED-CI® Silver

LIGHT, STRUCTURE, FLOW: Describing the store's breakthrough design, VM+SD (Visual Merchandising and Store Design) hailed REI-Seattle as a "space reflecting the beauty and austerity of nature, a customer-first orientation and an environmental commitment that included using as many recycled materials as possible, as economically as possible."

REI DENVER FLAGSHIP
Denver, Colorado

It is unmistakably REI's – and just as unmistakably the work of Mithun.

Transforming the 100-year-old Denver Tramway Power Company Building into an outdoor equipment retail store was nothing short of remarkable. In addition to saving a threatened City of Denver Landmark, this complex restoration preserved the essential character of the building, improved its structural integrity and achieved significant environmental goals.

For fifty years, the massive brick building burned coal to generate electricity for Denver's entire streetcar system. It became a warehouse for International Harvester Company during the 1950s and later reopened in 1969 as the Forney Historic Transportation Museum. April 28, 2000 represented yet another new beginning when REI Denver opened for business as the co-op's fourth flagship store.

REI Denver's completed design and the surrounding site responds to the existing industrial nature of the building: celebrating and reusing found objects; incorporating salvaged, recycled and low-environmental-impact building materials; and relying on heating, cooling and lighting schemes that minimize the use of fossil fuels.

DESIGN OVERVIEW
Mithun's green strategies focused on re-use of the existing structure and the artful inclusion of REI's retail program within its historic context – all while carefully integrating new materials and technologies into the building. Major renovations addressed seventy-five thousand square feet of brick reconstruction, replacement of deteriorated wood windows, and concrete restoration and repair. Leaving the old Tramway Building's internal structure and systems exposed as finished surfaces, as well as recycling materials found on site, created a visual link to the project's origins.

Constructed in 1901, this late Victorian structure is an excellent example of American Industrial architecture of the early 20th Century. The building was essentially one giant room,

LANDMARK STATUS: Housed in the historic Tramway Power Company Building, this REI Flagship store is classic late-Victorian, Richardson-Romanesque architecture. Restoring this City of Denver landmark and National Preservation Honor Award winner has breathed new life into the building as a retail destination.

POWERHOUSE: Between 1901 and 1950, Denver's entire electric streetcar system was powered by the plant's steam-powered electric generators and furnaces – massive engines fed by tons of lignite coal daily and cooled by water from the nearby South Platte River.

housing large furnaces and steam-powered electric generators, its load-bearing brick walls rising fifty-five feet to the roof.

Additionally, the new REI property contributed significantly to Denver's goal of reclaiming an urban neighborhood in the Central Platte Valley (CPV) – a brownfield zone targeted for redevelopment by the city in the 1980s. As a result of successful cleanup efforts, Denver's lower downtown district (LoDo) now includes a major amusement park, aquarium, Coors Field, the Pepsi Center Arena – and REI's Denver Flagship Store.

INTEGRATED DESIGN PROCESS

The design team's mission from the beginning was how to turn this historic structure into a functioning, sustainable retail environment – and do it cost effectively. Bert Gregory, Mithun's lead designer and a Denver native, recalled:

> It's an artifact, a treasured building that we had to respect because of its importance in history – not only the history of the trolley barn, but architecturally at a pivotal point in time in the formation of Colorado. So as we engaged the design process it was obvious we had to be careful with our interventions. To be very clear between what's new and what's old. To restore or replace elements without being historically false. And, always, to keep the bones of the building intact so that a hundred years from now, with proper maintenance, it could endure.

Early in the process, Mithun assembled a strong group of stakeholders representing REI, the Mayor's office, planning, building and fire department officials, and neighborhood and community groups. Local and state historic preservation experts identified key funding opportunities. They were joined by architectural, structural and construction consultants who were instrumental in discovering potential design and construction challenges. The Denver Urban Renewal Authority (DURA), the Colorado Historical Society and the National Park Service also provided crucial support.

Again, REI members were asked for input on developing the Denver Flagship. They responded by identifying top design priorities such as energy efficiency, alternative transit options, water conservation and sustainable building operating principles such as recycling. And like REI Seattle, the co-op made a commitment to build the store consistent with their corporate conservation ethic, to create a warm, inviting retail environment while ensuring financial accountability on behalf of the membership.

THE SITE

Redeveloping the five-acre site to complement the recycled building was central to achieving REI's conservation goals. The Denver Tramway Power Company Building was originally chosen for its proximity to downtown and today preserves a gateway view to the city for drivers traveling along Interstate 25. At the same time, the store's location next to the Platte River was ideal for conveying its outdoor recreation mission to urban dwellers.

The design team created a landscaped courtyard and store entry that visually extends the public park system along the south edge of the Platte and restores a vital connection to the river. This public green

OF HISTORIC PROPORTIONS: The Pinnacle, the store's featured 55-foot-high climbing rock, towers over several interactive specialty shops on two levels. REI-Denver welcomed one million visitors in 2001, its first full year of operation.

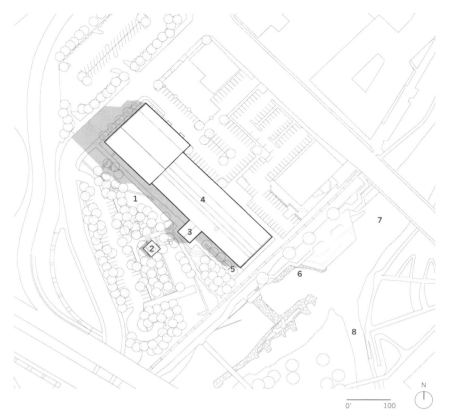

INSPIRED REDEVELOPMENT: From its origins as a turn-of-the-century powerhouse and former brownfields site, REI Denver has become a major attraction for outdoor enthusiasts across the Mountain States.

1 bicycle test trail
2 access tower to parking below
3 entry
4 historic tramway powerstation
5 cafe/porch
6 kayak test course
7 south platte river
8 cherry creek

THE GATEWAY: The new REI site and landscaped courtyard – not far from Denver's LoDo (Lower Downtown) District – visually extends the public park system along the south edge of the Platte River. The five-acre site is made up primarily of native Colorado Ponderosa and Lodgepole pine, Blue spruce, aspen, cottonwood, birch, alder, dogwood, juniper, kinnickinnick – and Pikes Peak granite.

space is adjacent to major bike path routes and a whitewater kayak course at Confluence Park, where shoppers can try out paddling products. It also serves a critical store function as a testing site for boots, shoes and bicycles. A grove of cottonwoods surrounds the store's outdoor bouldering wall, and the three hundred-eighteen-foot mountain bike test track winds through alders and birch trees.

More than sixty-two thousand square feet of new native Colorado plantings were introduced here: ponderosa and lodgepole pine, blue spruce, serviceberry, dogwood, juniper and kinnickinnick, as well as perennial flowers that include pasqueflower, forget-me-not and primrose. Drought-resistant gramma grass is the primary ground cover. The landscaping rock is Pikes Peak granite, reclaimed from the site of an abandoned dam blowout.

Another key decision was to construct a forty thousand-square foot underground garage beneath the public entry courtyard. This space serves a dual purpose of retaining the store's historic character and maintaining the view to downtown. Moving half of its total parking space underground also helps to limit heat islands and reduces the amount of impervious paving.

THE PROGRAM
The Denver store includes five specialty shops on two levels for climbing, camping, skiing, paddling and cycling. The old generator room of the 100- by 400-foot building features a seventy foot high vaulted ceiling. Within this space, the design team inserted a mezzanine level that hugs one wall while keeping the interior volume open as in the past. There are no escalators.

Specialty shops include in-store areas so customers can test and compare products: water filters and backpacking stoves; a bike light and reflector illumination station; a footwear test trail. A 6-by-8-foot titanium cold chamber was specially designed for testing and comparing cold-weather gear in temperatures to thirty degrees below zero. The store's centerpiece is the freestanding, forty-five foot tall "Pinnacle", its natural cracks and features designed to simulate a natural climbing environment. A 200-person auditorium, art gallery, café and child's play area, along with a repair shop, rental shop and store offices round out the design.

STRUCTURE & MATERIALS
Central to the building's re-design and restoration was material re-use, construction recycling and inclusion of recycled content wherever possible.

Much of the landmark's original structure was left intact: nearly five million bricks totaling seventy-five thousand square feet were tuckpointed; its steel structure utilized to support new floors inserted within the building shell; and existing interior elements – including stairs, smokestack structure and coal hoppers – were retained as historical artifacts. In addition, an existing steel water tank was cut up and reused for decorative signage accents and display panels throughout the facility. The team restored thirty original wood windows and created historic replicas for another 168 pieces that had deteriorated.

Salvaged materials from other locales also figured into the design. Reclaimed brick was used to repair and rebuild existing brick walls.

More than twenty-four thousand square feet of recycled wood decking for the new second floor structure came from an abandoned mine in Montana, as well as reclaimed wood timbers used to support the two main staircases. Flagstone discovered during site excavations made an ideal facing for the store's fireplace and was used to support the entrance to the parking garage.

Engineered wood panel products (MDF and OSB, from post-industrial waste) are used throughout the store for wall elements, cabinets and merchandise fixtures. Other materials containing high recycled content include countertops made of a soybean and newspaper composite and wood flooring from certified sustainable forest management practices. No old-growth timber products were harvested; instead, engineered lumber from new small diameter trees was manufactured into glue-laminated beams to imitate the look of larger timbers.

ENERGY

REI Denver was designed to operate using 30 percent less electricity than mandated by Colorado building energy codes. This target was achieved through evaporative cooling, natural daylighting tied to a photocell control system, efficient light fixtures, lighting motion detectors, and a computer-controlled energy management system. All windows now feature energy efficient low-e glass in double-pane insulated units.

HEATING & COOLING

The building's mechanical system relies on direct/indirect evaporative water-cooling to reduce energy consumption during summer months. Energy savings also result from greater temperature spread performance requirements and variable speed HVAC fans, allowing temperature variances of up to 5 degrees off optimum within the store.

LIGHTING & DAYLIGHTING

Natural daylighting illuminates more than one-fourth of the building's footprint. The store features high-efficiency metal halide and fluorescent lighting – with a photocell control system that continually adjusts the balance of ambient light throughout. Motion sensors detect occupancy for after-hours lighting. High-efficiency sodium vapor lighting is used in garage areas.

INDOOR AIR

The garage includes carbon monoxide sensors that activate exhaust fans when needed. The store's indoor air quality benefits from minimal use of coatings and stains on steel, wood structures and paneling – a decision that contributes to the building's raw, industrial look. Finishes were removed in some areas to eliminate potential off-gassing. Exterior treated timbers and shoring lagging utilized environmentally-friendly low VOC preservatives.

WATER

The store's landscaping relies on a high-efficiency, subsurface irrigation system to reduce water consumption. New bioswales were designed and constructed for water quality treatment. Inside, the public restrooms include low-flow and electronically-controlled plumbing fixtures to conserve water.

"Like the confluence of the South Platte River and Cherry Creek...different but compatible streams have come together – public and private; consumer and conservator; historic and au courant – to thoughtfully reuse a structure from the past for a wholly new function."

—2002 Awards for Excellence, the Urban Land Institute

A PERFECT FIT: With the strong emphasis on connections, re-use and recycling of materials throughout the store, it made sense to incorporate flagstone discovered during excavation of the parking garage. The fireplace in the Trip Planning Center has a distinctive iron chimney along with the flagstone facing.

New skylights were added to bring in more natural daylight. Photocells measure the natural light level and send signals to the building management computer to dim the lights accordingly. This daylight harvesting along with the indirect/direct evaporative cooling system help to reduce the energy consumption by up to 30 percent.

1 entry
2 existing steel structure
3 preserved interior volumes
4 new daylighting skylights
5 restored brick bearing walls
6 evaporative cooling based air conditioning
7 photo-sensors for daylight harvesting

EXTENDING THE BRAND: After opening its first international store in suburban Tokyo, Japan, REI's Portland, Oregon Flagship (pictured) became the first retail store in the U.S. to earn LEED-CI® Gold in 2004; two years later, the Co-op's Pittsburgh store earned LEED-CI® Silver.

PRINCIPLE 3

USE NATURE AS A GUIDE

WOODLAND PARK ZOO

"The roof changes dramatically from spring to summer to fall: brown to green to gold. Our design response was to create a very strong, open connection between the forest and interior exhibits – to blur that line between inside and outside literally using nature as the educational guide."

—Brendan Connolly, AIA, Mithun

WOODLAND PARK ZOO

Seattle, Washington

May 2006

"Native northwest forest meadow lifted to the sky"

It is a place that changes with the seasons – a created place, dramatizing the cycle of life, death, rebirth. The vegetated roof over Seattle's LEED® Gold Zoomazium features more than twenty thousand plants (grasses, ferns, flowers) native to the Puget Sound region and a six-inch layer of soil that simulates a Northwest forest floor. This roof is also a thriving habitat for microbes, insects and bird life. The 8,300-square-foot building itself is a purpose-built, "naturalistic" play space recently added to the Woodland Park Zoo to connect kids and their parents to the wonders of nature.

With the Zoo organized into a series of bioclimatic regions, this area represents the native Northwest temperate biome – so it only made sense to recreate a forest floor edge/meadow for all the world to see. Zoomazium's roof system also serves as a reminder of the building's sustainable focus: to keep its temperature constant, mitigate storm water, and create habitat. Seattle Public Utilities and the Zoo continue to measure the roof's performance (weather monitoring, soil temperature, storm water runoff, water quality, and wind microclimate data) over a two-year period to assess the viability of future green roof projects.

For Mithun, using nature as a guide is a premise central to the firm's growing body of work in building, interior and landscape design and master planning. In the Northwest, Mithun's design signature has long been nature – true to form, raw, respectful, responding to time and location. It becomes the shape of buildings to reflect the geology of a site. Or solar meadows as a clearing in the forest to optimize the performance of PV arrays. Or a street design that mimics the natural drainage of a pristine landscape.

Can we understand how to use nature from an ecological or ecosystems standpoint? And what does that teach us in designing our buildings and communities?

Using the natural forces on a site informs a neighborhood, campus or building architecture in a way that is at once sensory, biophilic, experiential. And presenting those forces – whether wind, water, sun, geology or vegetation – makes it somehow more authentic, focused, reinforcing the story of a place.

Nature minimizes toxicity. Reduces demand. Illustrates the natural progression of a community. Expresses materiality. It is science that helps to make those connections: of the nutrient cycle, the interface between aquatic and terrestrial habitats, water evaporation and transpiration. It is design that interprets how a developed place can function in a forest or an upland valley or an urban high-rise. The process to reach that understanding, too, is guided by nature – through resource modeling, the percolation rates of soil, analysis of building materials. Ultimately, it is an interdisciplinary team, with experts, that offers the best design insight: interdependent, comprehensive, thinking like an ecosystem.

CHAPTER 5:
HIGH POINT

INTRODUCTION

RE-IMAGINING PLACE, A NEW VISION OF COMMUNITY

"We wanted to create a neighborhood that feels special, with character that empowers its residents and on a scale that makes it fun to be there. Yet it was also important to design in a way that is reflective of the place: How do you relate homes to one another as far as light and solar access? How do you handle stormwater above a salmon-spawning stream without denigrating the value of that stream? Seeing all of these ideas together, I think, is where we are educating the future."

—William Kreager, FAIA, Mithun

"The street is the river of life of the city, the place where we come together, the pathway to the center."
William H. Whyte

From the city's highest point, it is easy to see Mount Rainier on a clear day — as well as the Olympic Range to the west or downtown Seattle on the far side of Elliot Bay. While the views here are magnificent, this place is equally impressive for what is on the ground: a new neighborhood filled with colorful housing, mature trees, parks, ponds and gardens. When complete, High Point will be the largest sustainable, mixed-income, urban community ever built in the United States.

It was not long ago that High Point was a very different place: a crime-ridden public housing project full of dilapidated, barracks-like structures dating back to World War II. In 2004, the Seattle Housing Authority (SHA) began razing the development as part of an ambitious project to start over, to reconnect this hilltop neighborhood with West Seattle. As lead planner and designer, Mithun went further still, beyond green design or new urbanism: seeing High Point as a new model for affordable, sustainable living.

ACTIVE PLACES: Mithun's master plan for High Point pairs many sustainable and new urbanist elements, creating active streetscapes throughout the community. Front porches become "eyes on the street", overlooking pocket parks and children's play areas. Pervious sidewalks are made of compressed, crushed concrete to reduce runoff, while narrow streets with natural curbs are paved with porous concrete. In between are shallow, landscaped swales, part of a natural drainage system that collects and filters rainwater.

HIGH POINT COMMUNITY
Seattle, Washington

Together, Mithun and SHA have completely transformed the sixty-year-old subsidized housing project into a vibrant, newly-thriving community for more than four thousand people with varied economic, ethnic and social backgrounds. With thirty-four city blocks spread across one hundred-twenty acres, High Point's energy-efficient houses, townhouses, apartments and condominiums will also serve as a national example for healthy homebuilding.

From the start, sustainability was a clear priority: to preserve mature trees, include transit-oriented measures, ensure good indoor air quality for occupants with asthma or serious allergies. In this once-blighted neighborhood, all housing types are designed to meet Seattle's Built Green™ 3-Star standards. Also put in motion was a plan to protect Longfellow Creek, a productive salmon habitat, with a community-wide natural drainage system (NDS) that directs storm water into a network of grassy swales.

Mithun's innovative master planning demonstrates how sustainability, urbanism, green infrastructure and architecture can be applied broadly in the housing industry. Here is a development that more than doubles its density and population, advances the market demand for green living, and substantially reduces the energy and water footprint of a growing community.

DESIGN OVERVIEW
High Point was conceived as a radically new approach to mixed income and sustainable communities. As the project developer, SHA is a public corporation providing affordable housing to twenty-four thousand people throughout the city. Mithun collaborated closely with the agency and community stakeholders to lead the planning process and include as many sustainable design practices as feasible in redeveloping the site and new home construction.

The master plan is designed to re-knit High Point into the surrounding West Seattle neighborhood and reduce reliance on automobiles. Its design intent emphasizes site ecology, contextual design, energy efficiency and resident health as well as new urbanist approaches to walkable, vibrant communities.

COMMUNITY GARDEN: Special attention was paid to active amenities like the neighborhood's Market Garden P·Patch, where residents can grow and sell their vegetables, as well as community gardens for about 10 percent of households.

"When it comes to residential development, few cities have the opportunity to reinvent 120 acres from the ground up, implement the most enlightened thinking about the environment, and plan ahead for sustainable energy consumption all at the same time. That's what makes Seattle's High Point so exciting."

—*Edens Lost & Found, PBS*

To create a strong sense of community, most of High Point's buildings sit within fifteen feet of narrow, pedestrian-friendly streets designed to slow traffic and encourage people to stop and chat. Porches oversee small pocket parks so parents and caregivers can easily monitor children playing outside. A mosaic of open spaces and playgrounds links people to the place and to each other.

Mithun provided design guidelines for all builders involved with the project. Five private developers then chose from among a palette of eleven complementary colors and twenty-seven building designs selected by SHA. All High Point home designs, even the community itself, aim for BuiltGreen™ 3-Star certification or better through the King and Snohomish County Master Builders Association. Homes, apartments and condos are expected to achieve at least 15 percent energy-and-water savings over conventionally-designed buildings through the use of double-pane windows, daylighting strategies, super-tight building envelopes, and resource-efficient fixtures and appliances. The final designs also reflect Seattle City Light Built SmartSM incentives and Energy Star Homes Northwest certification.

INTEGRATED DESIGN PROCESS

High Point neighborhood planning began in earnest in 2001. Mithun, consultants and SHA together formulated a strategy for the entire development, including a new street grid, underground utilities and parks. They also worked closely with Seattle Public Utilities, Seattle City Light and SvR, the civil engineers charged with designing the natural stormwater management strategy.

From the start, the design team also engaged residents as well as elected officials, planning staff and many civic leaders and businesses in the process of "placemaking." Surveys were used to gather broad input on the long-term impacts and needs of the area and its multicultural residents. Community meetings led to new ideas for shaping High Point as a home for people of all ages, cultures and financial means while informing the final neighborhood layout. With the help of interpreters spanning a dozen languages, these gatherings were used to ensure that all stakeholders were equally invested in the concept of a sustainable community.

Collaborative charrettes also guided the selection of designs for homes and community buildings. Residents asked that rental units feature distinctive façades to look like private homes. Other key themes emerged as well during the planning meetings, including: architectural variety and house-scaled fronts; accessibility; usable front yard space; comfortable front porches; and large windows. The need for security consistently rated high for tenants. As a result, the master plan features narrow, 25-foot-wide streets to foster slower driving speeds, a quieter neighborhood and a strong sense of community.

SHA's funding strategy leveraged public and private investments to raise the capital needed for a mixed-income development. Sixty percent of the housing budget came from private sources, including land sales, affordable housing tax credits, and capital investments.

The new High Point is a "HOPE VI" project, part of a nationwide effort inaugurated by HUD to redevelop troubled public housing developments into healthy mixed-income communities. The development's social equity approach is key to the overall strategy of a diverse neighborhood with green housing accessible to all levels of income. The eight-

ONCE UPON A TIME: The original High Point development sprouted up in the early 1940s when more than 700 one-story 'ramblers' were built to house defense plant workers who flooded Seattle to work for Boeing and the booming shipyards in support of the war effort.

hundred rental units at High Point, in fact, make up the largest single collection of Energy Star-certified homes in the nation. In addition, smart decisions about design details and appliances and partnerships among several city agencies made it possible for the subsidized market to participate.

THE SITE

Set on a peninsula approximately six miles southwest of downtown, West Seattle is surrounded by the Duwamish Waterway and Puget Sound. At High Point, designers saw a unique opportunity to integrate the neighborhood's land use and geography with habitat strategies and site ecology.

Central to the plan is that the re-designed community becomes a single, integrated natural drainage system – interconnected with parks, children's play areas, and landscaped drainage swales (disguised as planting strips between the sidewalks and streets) that collect rainwater runoff from impervious surfaces. High Point's stormwater pond is at the heart of a park with a quarter-mile walking trail, terraced lawn and overlook. A hillside greenbelt comprising the eastern edge of the site was left with its natural forest cover intact.

Habitat, community and site ecology were also factors in the decision to preserve a significant number of trees. The design team enlisted an arborist to assess the value of healthy specimens and established financial incentives to protect those trees from damage during construction. Approximately one hundred-fifty large, legacy trees were left in place – mostly evergreens – valued at more than $1.5 million. Wherever possible, the planners then developed the streets and

housing layout around the trees. It is expected that by the end of the project an additional eleven hundred new trees will be planted along High Point streets, with another two thousand new trees planned for parks, yards and open spaces.

THE PROGRAM

High Point's one hundred-twenty acres makes it one of the largest HOPE VI redevelopment projects in the country. Eventually this neighborhood will encompass seventeen hundred new market-rate and rental homes and feature a variety of public amenities and parks as part of a mixed-income, multi-generational community.

The redevelopment was divided into two phases, covering the northern half (Phase I) and southern half (Phase II) of the property. As in previous Seattle Housing Authority HOPE VI projects, the goal was to complete the low-income housing before allowing private builders to buy lots for their market homes.

Options at High Point include detached houses, duplexes, townhouses, condominiums and apartments – with each block featuring a mix of subsidized and market rate homes. All layouts typically feature open floor plans and large windows for good daylight penetration and natural ventilation. Because public transportation use is expected to be significantly higher than average, most housing is clustered in configurations only a fraction of a mile from bus stops.

Affordable housing at High Point was created expressly for very low-income or low-income individuals and working families who earn, respectively, 30 percent or less, 60 percent or less, and 80 percent

HIGH DENSITY, OPEN SPACE: The new High Point has become a national model for mixed income and sustainable communities. Its urban housing design virtually doubles the number of residents while significantly increasing the number of parks and playgrounds – totaling more than twenty acres of open space.

or less of the Seattle area median income (AMI). In early 2008, the AMI figure stood at approximately $56,000. The process to develop market-rate housing was very different. Typically, SHA leases land to nonprofit groups or sells land to developers while coordinating for-sale marketing efforts.

All community facilities are located within walking distance of the new housing and strategically located near the perimeter of the neighborhood to attract clientele from outside High Point. Major additions to the neighborhood include a new public library, dental and medical clinic, small retail center with a grocery and other shops, and the just-expanded High Point Community Center and its adjacent large ball fields. Also centrally located will be an expanded neighborhood center to house community meeting rooms, social services, job assistance programs, and classrooms for various study programs. The modern High Point Elementary accommodates students in a school central to the community.

High Point also features twenty acres of open space, including many small pocket parks, playgrounds, a network of paths and trails, and a large, five-acre central commons park in the middle of the development. Completing the plan are community garden spaces for about 10 percent of the households, as well as a market garden where residents can grow and sell their produce.

STRUCTURE & MATERIALS

Deconstruction and waste management were critical elements of the project even before construction began.

NEW MODEL FOR AFFORDABLE, SUSTAINABLE LIVING

Design goals for the High Point redevelopment included:

Maintain housing affordability with a variety of designs attractive to diverse ages, incomes and household types and sizes – and include a wide range of prices and types of for-sale housing.

Create a neighborhood that provides residents with places for gathering and learning, along with opportunities to celebrate their ethnic and cultural diversity.

Encourage development that protects health and maintains environmental quality.

Promote alternative ways of getting around, such as transit ridership, walking and bicycling.

Maximize use of natural systems to clean water and control stormwater runoff.

Indicative of what we need to do with our old building stock to meet climate protection needs, High Point's 1600 new homes now using less total energy than the 700 that were replaced.

—*Tammie Sueirro Schacher, AIA, Mithun*

Although the old, deteriorated buildings on the Phase I property had to be removed, SHA saw an opportunity to salvage many of the materials. Twenty-two original High Point buildings were carefully dismantled by hand – preserving Items such as siding, drywall and electrical outlets – and recycled for use in new home kitchens and baths. Deconstruction teams were also able to recover nearly 90 percent of the old-growth framing, plywood, flooring and other lumber for reuse and sale.

Several additional measures were taken to minimize the amount of construction and demolition waste as part of High Point's sustainability goals. These measures included: stockpiling and reusing existing topsoil; reusing old paving as backfill in trenches; and reusing crushed concrete foundations and sidewalks in the street base. Neighborhood trees slated for removal were reused on site for furniture, benches, trail markers, trellis posts, signage, play features, habitat restoration and mulch.

Because one-half of the development is designated for families with low and modest incomes, the project team has been careful to employ sustainable materials and strategies where it makes economic sense. Low-allergen, drought-tolerant plants, zero-VOC paint, and energy-efficient appliances cost no more than standard options. Walls are panelized for maximum resource efficiency; advanced framing was guided by optimum value engineering strategies such as stacked framing and 24-inch stud spacing.

Rapidly renewable and reclaimed wood products were used whenever possible. High Point houses also feature tankless water heaters, flat-panel radiators, double glazed low-e vinyl windows, hydronic heating systems, R-19 walls, R-38 roofs, porous concrete, and R-10 rigid insulation under slabs.

ENERGY
All homes at High Point meet the local Built Green™ 3-Star standard that encourages practical innovations and energy efficiency. The resulting units are affordable, well insulated and well ventilated – and designed to exceed state energy code requirements by 15 to 20 percent.

With the assistance of Seattle City Light, Mithun performed energy modeling using E-quest (DOE 2-based). The specifications for homes and all rental units called for Energy Star-rated fans, lighting and appliances to further reduce energy costs. The outdoor fluorescent fixtures feature daylight sensors.

HEATING & COOLING
Home designs feature gas-fired tankless water heaters to supply radiant baseboard heaters. This approach allows each room to be heated individually, essentially avoiding standby losses and reducing heating bills. The tankless water heaters also provide the domestic hot water. Additionally, a passive ventilation strategy is tied to a timer-controlled bath fan, which serves as the whole house fan and operates fiftenn minutes every hour. Makeup air is brought in through wall vents located in all rooms.

Air sealing measures (based on the Airtight Drywall Approach) include insulated headers, corners, at-wall intersections and windows with

Longfellow Creek
Greenbelt

NATURAL SYSTEMS

The community's density — 14 to 36 units per acre — is not ideal for traditional drainage systems that replace gutters with shallow swales. The solution was to create deep drainage swales that look like the planting strips historically found between sidewalks and streets. Instead of being crowned, the streets tilt toward the planting strips.

- vegetated swale
- shallow swale
- conveyance swale

LAND USE

The neighborhood integrates the market rate and subsidized housing with distributed park systems and a network of streets that connect to the surrounding neighborhood.

- civic/parks
- market rate
- subsidized
- 1 pocket parks
- 2 neighborhood park system
- 3 commons park
- 4 High Point park
- 5 High Point Elementary

WATER FLOW

The community's natural drainage system aims to protect a critcal creek for salmon habitat. The streets are narrow to reduce runoff, while rain that falls on pavement and roofs flows into planted areas and slowly infiltrates into the groundwater. Drainage swales imitate tradtional planting strips, using both lawn and native shrubs. Some sidewalks and one street are made of porous concrete to let water through. Excess rain runs into a pond in a park at the community's north end.

- civic/parks
- water flow

CREATING HIGH POINT

2001:   Master Planning for redevelopment begins

PHASE 1 DEVELOPMENT: (NORTHERN HALF)

July 2004:   Infrastructure construction begins
September 2004: Low-income rental housing construction begins
July 2005:   First group of low-income residents move into
                              units
September 2005: For-sale housing construction begins
April 2006:   First group of homebuyers move into units
June 2006:   All low-income rentals complete and occupied
Mid 2008:   For-Sale homes sold out

PHASE 2 DEVELOPMENT: (SOUTHERN HALF)

July 2006:   Infrastructure construction begins
September 2007: Low-income rental housing construction begins
June 2008:   First group of low-income residents move into
                              units
March 2009:   For-sale housing construction begins
June 2009:   All low-income rentals complete and occupied
Late 2009:   First group of homebuyers move into units
Late 2011:   For-Sale homes sold out

LONGFELLOW'S RESTORATION: Adjacent to
the neighborhood, Longfellow Creek is one of
the three largest natural streams left in Seattle
and among the city's most productive for Coho
salmon. The health of High Point and the creek
are intertwined, as the development makes up
about 10 percent of its watershed. As a result,
excess storm water is directed into grassy swales
throughout the community and a retention pond
before flowing into the creek.

average U-values below .33 to meet Built SmartSM requirements. These envelope improvements are projected to save another 7.5 to 15 percent in heating and cooling costs beyond Washington State code.

LIGHTING & DAYLIGHTING

All homes incorporate daylighting strategies and energy efficient lighting to decrease energy consumption and reduce maintenance costs.

INDOOR AIR

In addition, sixty of the low-income residences are Breathe Easy™ homes, designed to improve indoor air quality through better tightness and ventilation. High Point is the first community in the country, in fact, to offer these housing units built specifically for families with asthma-related health problems. Based on recent studies showing that asthma disproportionately affects low-income housing occupants, the team wanted to address potential respiratory issues through home design and selection of materials.

The completed Breathe Easy™ residences feature easy-to-clean surfaces such as linoleum flooring and window blinds, hydronic heating and enhanced ventilation systems. Paints, finishes, adhesives, sealants and cabinetry all feature no or low VOCs. The insulated windows and foundations are designed to minimize dust, humidity and moisture. Even the landscaping features non-allergenic plants chosen to cut down on the release of pollen.

WATER

The High Point neighborhood comprises approximately 10 percent of the Longfellow Creek Watershed, which then flows to the Duwamish River and on to Puget Sound.

All thirty-four blocks of the project have been incorporated into the largest natural drainage system in the U.S. To maximize the landscape's role in treating runoff and protecting water quality, the one hundred-twenty acre site essentially functions like an open meadow: water is cleaned, cooled and filtered through the ground before it reaches the creek. The new drainage system is expected to reduce runoff flowing into Longfellow Creek by 80 percent compared to a conventional stormwater approach. In contrast, the old neighborhood's gutters and drainage pipes carried high volumes of stormwater – containing dirt, oil, pesticides and other pollutants – from rooftops, streets and sidewalks directly to the creek.

High Point's engineered stormwater drainage system begins with the houses, channeling the roof runoff through splashblocks and drains to furrows and channels. Community right-of-way design is central to directing rainwater and minimizing runoff. Narrow streets slope gently to one side, discharging water through cut curbs into four miles of grassy and vegetated swales throughout High Point. To minimize the need for irrigation and use of pesticides, designers selected native drought-tolerant plants for landscaping; soils were amended to improve water retention.

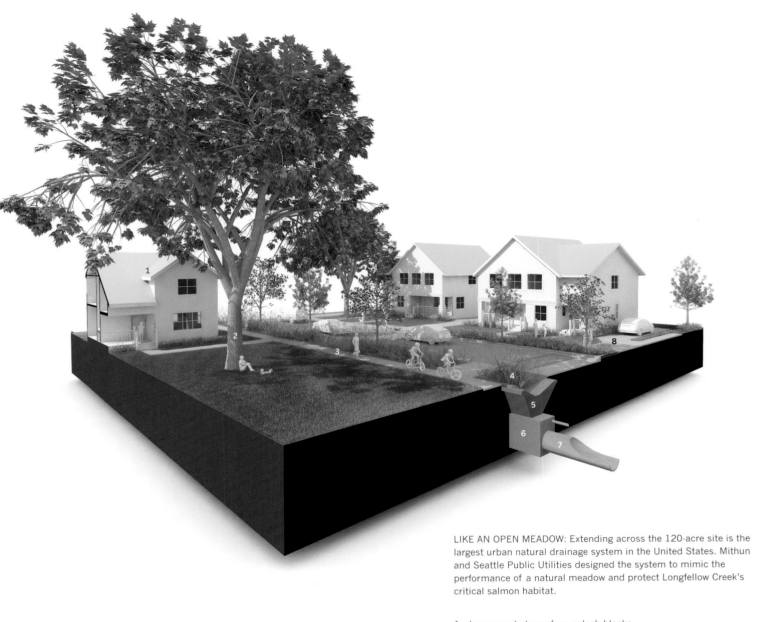

LIKE AN OPEN MEADOW: Extending across the 120-acre site is the largest urban natural drainage system in the United States. Mithun and Seattle Public Utilities designed the system to mimic the performance of a natural meadow and protect Longfellow Creek's critical salmon habitat.

1 down spouts to surface splash blocks
2 existing mature tree
3 porous concrete sidewalks
4 vegetated swale
5 NDS Engineered Soil Mix
6 aggregate pipe bed
7 storm sewer
8 gravel pavement

LEXIS ON THE PARK:
"A metaphor for upscale, sustainable, urban renaissance"

On the site of an old rail yard in northwest Portland is a vision realized: a lifestyle-focused condominium community that is transforming an area of abandoned warehouses, empty offices and an unused railroad track into an energized, welcoming urban neighborhood. Lexis on the Park, for Hoyt Street Properties, features street-level retail and five stories of luxury studio, one- and two-bedroom apartments, as well as live/work spaces and spacious town homes with private terraces. Mithun's design is clean and contemporary while reflecting the strong industrial origins of this district. Above its white concrete base, the block-long structure is wrapped in perforated aluminum and welded stainless steel mesh. Elegant detailing includes glass tiles, upper-story setbacks and metal sun screens that project over the top. The centerpiece of the building's design is a raised central courtyard – an open,

outdoor space for residents – and an adjacent plaza that serves as a transportation hub for pedestrians, bicyclists and those waiting for the Central City trolley line.

Experiencing Lexis on the Park begins to the west with the city's new Tanner Springs Park, then crossing over the streetscape, past a light-rail station, and entering a series of mixed-use retail shops. This progression from public to private space concludes with the plaza and interior courtyard of the Lexis. Mithun's lively, high-density urban design for this transit-oriented development has proven already to be a key element of Portland's long-term strategy to revitalize the Pearl District.

Lexis on the Park, Portland, Oregon

July 2005

Five-story, retail/multi-family full block urban infill development, 120,000 square feet (including below grade parking), 139 units, part of Portland's long-term redevelopment strategy for the Pearl District, enhancing connections to the adjacent park to re-weave fragments of Portland's urban eco-system by reclaiming Montana Creek.

2006 NAHB Best For-Sale Community of the Year: more than 40 units per acre, 2006 Builder's Choice Award

"I love the Pearl District. There's something about the scale of Portland's city blocks – they're small and respond on all sides to these wonderful streetscapes. From a materiality and design standpoint, Lexis on the Park relates very well to its surroundings, taking advantage of the future transit line. The building is also an appropriate answer to the park, itself a little jewelbox of sustainability. I think its relationship to the public realm is exactly what it needed to do."

—Jim Bodoia, AIA, Mithun

MOSLER LOFTS:
"Bright lights, big city, green living"

If Seattle is celebrated as a place for healthy, green living, then Mosler Lofts is the perfect setting to showcase sustainability as an urban lifestyle choice. Located in the city's Belltown District – full of hip eateries and nightlife – this twelve-story condo development, for the Schuster Group, features two-story townhouses, flats, penthouses and a ground-floor retail space and pedestrian-scale "green street" just steps from Seattle Center and the Olympic Sculpture Park. All units within Mosler Lofts were designed and conceived to emphasize openness, space, light and stunning views – and to feature materials that are raw and clean: ten-foot high concrete ceilings, exposed ductwork and floor-to-ceiling glass. The tower, wrapped in steel, glass and concrete, emerges from its four-story brick base, then continues to step back – respecting the scale and character of this historic neighborhood. Water, air

and energy are also critical elements here. A green roof terrace filters rainwater while also creating a gathering place for residents. Operable windows, large roof overhangs, recessed glazing areas, interior sun shades, and use of brick and concrete as thermal mass all contribute to reducing the building's energy load.

It is Seattle's first LEED® Silver residential high-rise. But more significant, perhaps, Mosler Lofts was the fastest selling condominium in the metro area's highly competitive marketplace during 2006. Together with the commitment of an inspired owner group, Mithun's design signals the start of a new era that green can be profitable in creating a 24/7 live-work community that appeals to urban professionals.

1 future proofed for photovoltaic panels
2 natural daylighting & views in all units
3 high performance window wall and glazing system
4 water conserving fixtures
5 regional material use
6 high efficiency chiller unit no cfc's
7 high efficiency elevator system
8 high efficiency boilers
9 rooftop recreation areas
10 green roof
11 energy star appliances
12 use of certified wood
13 enhanced commissioning systems
14 underground parking
15 flex car
16 bicycle storage & changing area
17 stormwater management
18 co_2 monitoring
19 recycling collection & storage area
20 evapo-transpiration
21 swale / water infiltration

Mosler Lofts, Seattle, Washington

December 2007

Retail/multi-family residential, 12 stories, 242,800 square feet (including below grade parking), 150 units

High-performance window wall and glazing system, natural daylighting, rooftop garden, high-efficiency chiller and boilers, water conserving fixtures, Energy Star® appliances, occupancy sensors for lighting and CO_2, sustainably harvested and recycled materials, water-efficient landscaping, storm water management, "green street" development

LEED® Silver and Built Green™, 2008 NAHB Multifamily Community of the Year

"Mosler Lofts is one of the strongest examples of Mithun's residential heritage with a sustainable point of view. It was done for a private developer, not an institution. It went green, not because the city, state or county offered any bonuses or incentives, but because it connected with what people wanted. The building generated a lot of buzz as an offering in Seattle – and I think that truly exemplifies the idea of enduring value in the market."

—Steve Cox, AIA, Mithun

VARIATION AND COLOR: Whether market-rate rentals or tax credit townhomes, the high-density housing at High Point is marked by its varied building designs and colors.

NATIVE, DROUGHT-TOLERANT: A network of grassy and vegetated swales handles storm water runoff across the street grid. Through use of site-suitable plants and amended soils, the swales allow water to percolate, acting as natural filters and improving water retention.

ART IN PUBLIC PLACES: A recycled cedar fence surrounds High Point's Market Garden – each board painted with a different design by a returning resident or local schools and businesses.

126

RENEWING A DREAM: High Point then and now, its grid of narrow, winding streets and sidewalks reconnects the neighborhood with the rest of West Seattle. Expanded open space includes a large storm water retention pond that forms the center of a park featuring trails, a children's playground, terraced lawn and overlook. Higher density resulted in 1,700 compact houses, townhouses and apartments – all while protecting the Longfellow Creek Watershed (foreground).

before

after

PRINCIPLE 4

CREATE BEAUTY AND SPIRIT

NOVELTY HILL-JANUIK WINERY

"Typically wineries refer back to some historic time or place. We wanted to convey a modern reverence for the wine and the craft of winemaking, to experience its taste from grape to glass. From the big idea of the building all the way down through the details, you feel that when you're here."

—Paul Wanzer, AIA, Mithun

NOVELTY HILL-JANUIK WINERY

Woodinville, Washington

June 2007

"A fine blend of science, nature, tradition and the senses"

"Inside out": the views in the building are open, airy, guided – from the winery's north end, where racks of French oak barrels are stored, to public tasting areas and through to the grand modern garden on the south. East-west walls to either side are largely transparent, overlooking a series of hillside terraces and the natural wetland beyond. The multi-story, 31,000-square-foot Novelty Hill-Januik Winery intentionally blurs the line between indoors and outdoors. Concrete floors in the production area become the concrete terrace outdoors. Interior walls align with exterior walls. Gardens flow seamlessly into private meeting rooms. Exposed beams extend the pattern of the tasting room's ceiling through a wall of glass windows

and to the canopy of ash trees outside. Mithun's integrated design won both an AIA National Honor Award for Interior Architecture and the International Interior Design Association Interior Design Award.

The winery's contemporary design celebrates its agrarian roots, a clear connection to the land that reflects an approach centered on biophilia. It is expressed by views to the sky and shadows that move throughout the day against the canvas of concrete walls. And by a warm southern light flooding every space within the building's massive concrete framework.

INTEGRATED DESIGN: MITHUN

It is the perfect moment. A sense of place, time and movement. Clear and deeply resonant. Beautiful design, for Mithun, is sustainable. And elegant, functional, dramatic, enduring. More than proportion and form, to "Create Beauty & Spirit" is a celebration of detail, design elements with purpose, relevant, that contribute to a greater whole. The living fence, a courtyard sculpture, daylight pouring through a wall, a salvaged, old-growth timber that tells a story – each a surprise in their discovery. Using the architecture of buildings to create outdoor spaces that invite waterfront or forest views. Transforming an empty streetscape into a place of belonging.

It is not a matter of which building is the most beautiful. We are trying to create something more meaningful out of what we are doing.

Intuitive yet steeped in science: how to connect site, building and interiors to living systems. Learning from history. Bringing the outside in, the inside out. Capturing the instant of an idea.

Beauty, meaning and spirit exist as a clearing in the forest. The pattern language of a neighborhood. The view across a restored wetland, again full of life, better than before. Through use of color. Sequential experience. Honesty of structure and materials. These ideals are central to the firm's natural progression into urban planning and design: influencing policy, creating places for people, changing perceptions and realities for the urban environment. And they remain part of the DNA of Mithun: blending expertise across disciplines, making the invisible visible, communicating the soul of a program.

CHAPTER 6:
NORDHEIM COURT & EPLER HALL

INTRODUCTION

LIVING GREEN ON CAMPUS
Student Housing at Nordheim Court & Epler Hall

"How might materials, light, sounds, water, spatial configuration, openness, scenery, colors, textures, plants, and animals be combined to enhance the range and depth of learning?"
David Orr, Earth in Mind

"We had just finished Nordheim Court in Seattle, and we always joked the final result could be equated to music or film, that it was the 'Moulin Rouge of student housing'. For PSU's Epler Hall, we wanted to create an 'Unplugged' version, with architecture that was extremely understated. To rely on proportion, composition and detailing, as opposed to the expressive color and vibrance and sculpturalism at Nordheim – and yet still express a message of sustainability."

—*Ron van der Veen, AIA. Mithun*

Hundreds of thousands of prospective college freshmen and transfers visit colleges every year. Just as more undergraduates are choosing to live on campus, their housing demands and expectations are increasingly more sophisticated. Students want more privacy. More space. And increasingly they want housing that is sustainable.

For Mithun, opportunities to create vital living/learning spaces that celebrate sustainability were realized for two northwest schools. The University of Washington's Nordheim Court succeeds as a European-style student village that is modern and environmentally intelligent. Likewise, the high-rise Stephen Epler Residence Hall at Portland State University is popular for its creative, interactive design features tied closely to the natural environment.

FOCAL POINT: Leading into the complex of eight buildings is the "Agora", Nordheim Court's central plaza and a popular gathering place. Large-scale sculpture such as "Antenna Reeds" is a defining feature of this urban village for University of Washington grad students.

NORDHEIM COURT, UNIVERSITY OF WASHINGTON

Seattle, Washington

Even beneath an overcast Seattle sky, it is bold, bright, unexpected – a student housing alternative that celebrates community while focusing on the natural environment and art. The contemporary design, colors and stunning artwork have made Nordheim Court a unique addition to the University Village neighborhood.

The University of Washington (UW) complex features townhouses above apartments, each accented with metal and color to create a modern interpretation of walk-up brownstones. Interspersed throughout the eight diverse buildings are outdoor spaces that connect – via terraced steps – to a pond and small forest-like setting of tall trees. In addition, this LEED® certified project emphasizes recycled products, low-VOC emitting materials, natural ventilation, daylighting, a highly insulated building envelope, porous concrete, drought-tolerant landscapes and roof water that recharges the existing pond.

Upon its completion in summer 2003, Nordheim Court was immensely popular with UW students and leased out in the first day. Equally significant, it represented strong, continuous collaboration among architects, staff, faculty and students, a collaboration that effectively balanced competing requirements for quality, affordability and good design.

DESIGN OVERVIEW

Mithun's integrated team set out to create an urban village within a suburban context – on a site that still retained much of its rural appearance. The three- and five-story buildings are arranged around a central plaza, a progression of courtyards and an existing pond. The result is a mix of unit types, building massing and green space designed to create an intimate community in this area of high urban density.

Nordheim Court's eight walk-up units are clad in contemporary shades of ochre, slate, lime and blue, the exteriors featuring a combination of zinc metal panels and beveled siding made of cementitious board that resembles wood. The courtyard treatments are varied: all student living areas overlook active, socially-oriented courtyards, while bedrooms and study areas face courtyards that are passive.

(oppostie) THE VILLAGE EFFECT: From its urban street edge and across the site to the east, Nordheim Court has a distinct modern European profile, an internal street opening onto a series of landscaped courtyards with terraced steps and a natural pond.

STUDENT HOUSING ALTERNATIVE: Much in demand among UW students, all walk-up units feature daylighting, natural ventilation, operable windows and other responsive design elements so residents can control their own indoor climates.

1 summer sun
2 winter sun
3 garage
4 pond integrated into public space

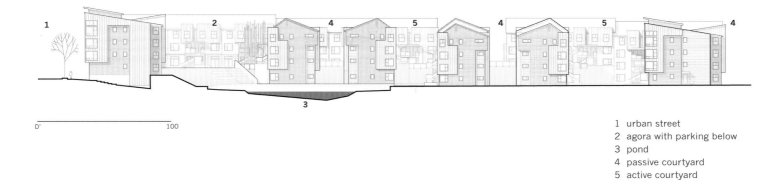

0' ———————— 100

1 urban street
2 agora with parking below
3 pond
4 passive courtyard
5 active courtyard

To further the feel of a modern European village, Mithun wanted to eliminate reliance on automobiles, not just mitigate their impact. Although city code mandated one hundred-fifty stalls for parking, Mithun suggested moving the parking structure underground. As a result, the buildings, courtyards and central plaza roll over the edge of a hidden parking deck. All walls were kept low, some areas built up subtly with larger plant material that further disguises the concrete structure and connects the entire apartment complex to the street nearby.

INTEGRATED DESIGN PROCESS
Increases in freshman class size at the University of Washington and a high rate of retention in residence halls led to an unexpected upsurge in requests for single-student housing in the early 2000s. To meet this demand, university planners called for an apartment-style residence hall to accommodate four hundred undergraduate and graduate students and community assistants in an off-campus setting north of Seattle's University Village shopping center.

Through a public/private partnership between UW's Department of Housing and Food Services (HFS), Lorig Management Services and Twenty-Fifth Avenue Properties, Mithun was commissioned to create this new undergraduate student housing complex to include 134 apartment units. Eco-charrettes held during pre-design brought together multiple stakeholders including the construction team, UW Engineering Services and Seattle City Light representatives. A team approach and early involvement by the developer, owner, architect, landscape architect and all consultants was critical to making sustainable choices throughout the project.

Cost management was also a clear, recurring theme during the

workshops. Because these housing projects are not subsidized by the university, it was important for the design to "pencil out": to create a great student housing environment with high architectural ambitions and yet adhere to a strict budget of eighty-five dollars per square foot in 2002 dollars. UW did not require LEED® certification, yet the designers and developer together identified potential LEED® credits as an effective way to benchmark its environmental performance during all phases of the project. With a construction budget of $20 million and a total development budget of $27.5 million, they agreed that the additional cost to achieve LEED® certification would be only $44,000 – or about 0.2 percent of total first costs.

THE SITE
Nordheim Court's low-rise buildings stand in sharp contrast to the large apartment blocks along the edge of the hill above Montlake Boulevard just a few blocks to the south. Even with its high density of fifty-two units per acre, there is both an urban and a rural way of moving through the site.

Starting at the west, the largest building forms a strong urban street edge, complete with entry stoops. A pedestrian street, flanked by stairs and planters, leads into the central plaza known as the "Agora", a popular gathering place. The main plaza then connects via terraced stairs to a small pond and mature tree canopy at the southwest side of the property. Once the site of a commercial landscape nursery, the trees were planted in the 1930s and 1940s; the pond was dug to access groundwater for watering. Nordheim's project team elected to preserve both features, removing only a few diseased trees and those within building footprints. In keeping with the project's sustainability goals, the pond naturally filters and retains storm water runoff.

"The Northwest landscape is revered. It's why people move here. They want to be out in nature. So to bring that experience into the city, to show all the different ways we can interact with the landscape in an urban place, is what Nordheim does."

—Deb Guenther, ASLA, Mithun

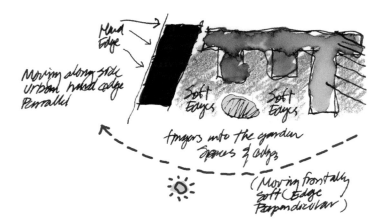

Continuing east across the site, the internal street opens onto a series of smaller, south-facing courtyards. All living areas focus on active spaces. Mithun also faced ground-level units outward to further activate the site and provide greater security as residents come in and out of their front doors on both sides. In contrast, the bedrooms and study areas concentrate on passive courtyards. The final courtyard, an open lawn bordered by trees, ends the procession with a variation of the first building and links with the bike path leading back to campus.

THE PROGRAM
The University of Washington originally designated four hundred beds for the site, envisioning a double-loaded corridor donut-type building typical of most dorms. But Mithun designers quickly illustrated how they could improve project density and quality of experience by creating a village scheme. The result is a variety of residences that offer vibrancy and choice. By reconfiguring the size and orientation of the buildings, and rigorously enforcing a hierarchy of public spaces, they were able to add an eighth building to the site, resulting in sixty more beds. The final layout includes 94-four bedroom, 32-two bedroom and twenty studio housing units, totaling four hundred-sixty beds.

To further manage costs, Mithun specified a standard package for the furnished bedrooms and living rooms, bathrooms, stairways, and fully equipped kitchens in all apartments. Two students share a bathroom. Some units feature loft spaces. To maximize efficiency, they reduced the size of the bedrooms but oversized the windows, making the space feel larger.

Much of the welcomed variety at Nordheim Court comes through color. Mithun created a palette of fall, spring and summer colors

HARD EDGES, SOFT EDGES: As part of its site analysis, Mithun used concept sketches, exploring potential hard edges and soft edges of the project, to inform the final layout.

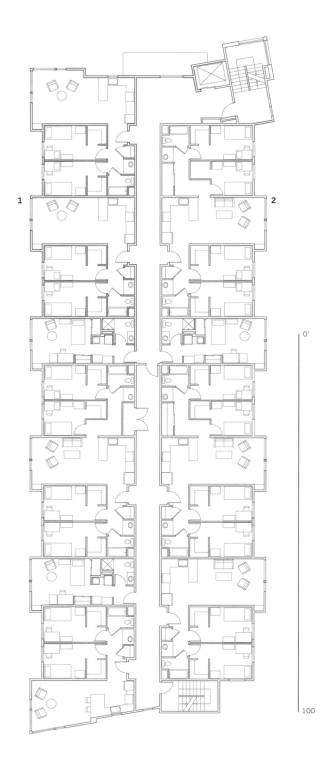

1

2

0'

100

FLOORPLAN: To increase project density, Mithun recommended that buildings incorporate walk-up units rather than pursue a double-loaded corridor design. The result is a range of seven to thirty apartments, townhouses and studio housing units per building.

1 typical 4-bedroom townhouse
2 typical 4-bedroom apartment

for the interior paint and fabrics throughout. The project's interior designer suggested extending this color scheme to the outside as well. Not only did this choice enliven the exteriors, it helps to identify buildings easily within the complex.

Ultimately, the project programming combines elements of undergraduate living with the amenities normally found in an apartment complex. Shared spaces include the 24-hour fitness center, a community room with full kitchen and media center, state-of-the-art laundry centers, and bike storage, as well as controlled-access underground parking.

STRUCTURE & MATERIALS
Using the LEED® calculator, 35 percent of all building materials at Nordheim Court contain recycled content. This content includes a high percentage of the insulation (30 percent) used in each building: R-21 in walls, R-38 in ceilings, loose fill in attics. In addition, fly ash was substituted for 43 percent of the cement in the architectural concrete. Locally harvested and manufactured materials were also a high priority. This local priority applies to 50 percent of all building materials, including lumber, fiber cement lap siding that resembles wood, gypsum wallboard, and vinyl windows.

ENERGY
As constructed, the Nordheim Court structures exceed Washington State Energy Code requirements by 30 percent. Upgraded insulation and passive solar design also qualified the project for financial incentives through the Seattle City Light BUILT SMART^{SM} program.

"We wanted the students here to be able to experience this housing development without ever interacting with an automobile. Most students will not use a car during the week; they will walk, take the bus or ride their bikes."

—*Ron van der Veen, AIA, Mithun*

HEATING & COOLING

In addition to upgrading the insulation, the buildings' solar positioning, zoned mechanical systems, and gas hot water boiler systems have combined to increase energy performance and lower utility bills.

LIGHTING & DAYLIGHTING

Nordheim Court was designed to emphasize natural light. Over-sized windows ensure that abundant daylight enters each unit on at least two sides. The large windows also serve to capture space from outside, making the compact units feel roomy. Tall, columnar trees planted in the plaza accentuate this effect by giving residents leafy views from their bedroom windows.

The rectangular buildings point south to maximize sun access; their southern, sculptural ends create opportunities for more windows – sending light into units on three sides, sometimes four, and even to the restrooms. During daylight hours, students typically do not need to turn on electric lights.

INDOOR AIR

To ensure high IAQ quality inside the buildings, Mithun specified only sealants, adhesives and paints with zero VOCs. Exterior paint products exceed Green Seal paint standard's G-11 requirement. All carpets used in Nordheim Court contain very low levels of VOCs and comply with the CRI Green Label Test Program.

The walk-up "through" units are naturally ventilated with operable windows. None of the buildings are double-loaded. Instead, the outdoor plazas serve as corridors for student mingling. Kitchens, living rooms

and dining rooms are all open to share fresh breezes and natural light.

WATER

To minimize impact on the site's hydrological cycle, combined water strategies achieve a 50 percent reduction in potable water use. Low-flow plumbing fixtures, including toilets and faucets, save substantial amounts of water compared to conventional fixtures. Drought-tolerant plantings dramatically cut irrigation requirements, while an existing pond was incorporated into the stormwater management system. Roofs channel rainwater into the pond, and a pervious footpath (the first porous sidewalk in Seattle) preserves its natural edge. Wildflower meadows between the buildings and a small sloped lawn for sitting require no irrigation.

OCCUPANT EDUCATION

Appropriate to its educational setting, the buildings at Nordheim Court serve as a learning environment in several ways. So that tenants operate energy management systems correctly while increasing their awareness of sustainable design, each student receives an information packet prior to leasing space.

To promote social sustainability, designers also developed strategies to encourage student interaction – particularly important for incoming freshmen. They devised one main route for entering and leaving the site that is flanked by common areas such as the mailroom and administrative office. Research, including security models and mapping view lines, further showed that the social interaction of stoops added to street-side entrances would more than offset any security risk.

VIBRANCY AND CHOICE: Nordheim Court's 3- and 5-story structures feature a mix of unit types, building massing and varied courtyard types – creating an intimate community in this area of high urban density.

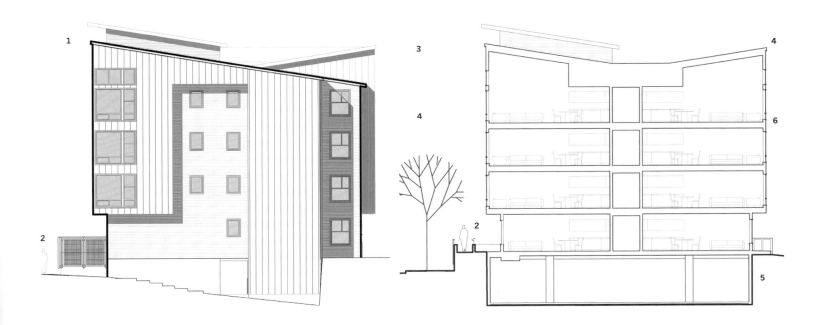

BUILDING 1 SOUTH ELEVATION

BUILDING 1 SECTION

1 urban edge
2 front stoop
3 urban street
4 agora
5 parking
6 units

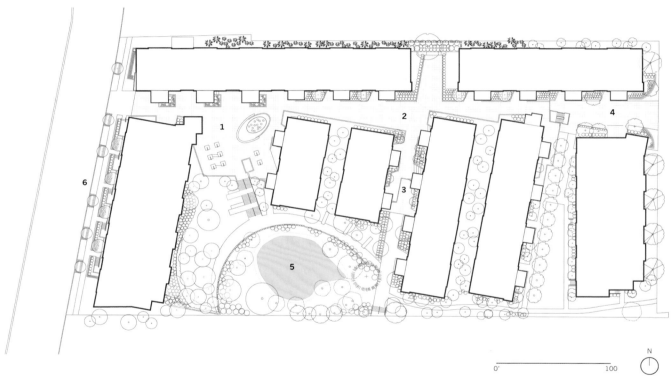

A SITE RESTORED, A PLACE FOR PEOPLE:
Mithun's plan for the 2.78-acre site resulted in a
preserved pond, private and public courtyards that
feature native plantings, a berm over underground
parking, and habitat restoration – all wrapped
around the north-south axis of student housing
with a mature tree canopy at its edges.

1 agora
2 "street"
3 passive plaza
4 active plaza
5 pond
6 urban street

0'   100

N

EVOLUTION OF IDEAS: Far from the norm for student housing, the complex represents a culmination of Mithun's design ideas developed over the past decade: a series of active and passive plazas; columnar trees for privacy; residence buildings clad in a contemporary palette of ochre, slate, lime and blue; and easy access to a nearby bike path to encourage alternative transportation. LEED® Certified, Nordheim Court is considered one of the firm's best examples to date of integrating interior design, landscape and architecture.

STEPHEN E. EPLER RESIDENCE HALL, PORTLAND STATE UNIVERSITY
Portland, Oregon

"We, the students, faculty, staff, and administration of Portland State University hereby commit to helping create a more sustainable world. We believe we must act now to address interconnected environmental, social and economic problems in this region, the nation, and abroad."

—*Declaration of Support for Sustainability at Portland State University*

"Portland State is...Diverse, Engaged, International, *Sustainable.*"

Perhaps nowhere is Portland State University's (PSU) commitment to campus sustainability more evident than with Stephen Epler Hall. Mithun's design of the six-story residence hall couples smart technology with climate-responsive design, taking full advantage of rainwater, daylight and natural breezes to assist the building's operation. Named after PSU's founding father, Stephen E. Epler, it is also the City of Portland's first mixed-use LEED Silver building.

In addition to high-quality student housing, the sixty-four thousand square-foot high-rise features classrooms, community spaces and offices. Construction of Epler Hall was completed in time for fall classes in 2003, and on the day it opened to students, all studio units quickly sold out.

PSU's "Declaration of Support for Sustainability" represents an array of initiatives in energy conservation, building design, native landscaping, waste reduction and stormwater management. For many, Epler Hall best exemplifies the shared values of sustainability among the student population, alumni, staff and administration that has been driving change both in campus facilities and its academic curricula over the past decade.

DESIGN OVERVIEW
As designed and built, Stephen E. Epler Hall successfully captures the natural benefits of air, rain and sun and carefully integrates energy conservation within the university's structure while increasing students' awareness and learning opportunities about natural resources.

Ron van der Veen, Mithun's lead designer, noted that the project's primary goal was to refine this rectangular building into a "smart structure" that responds to the micro-climates of each building's façade. Effectively, these "responsive façades" reflect its solar orientation and urban context by addressing wind, noise and views. The west side, for example, runs along an urban street and connects the building with its off-campus neighborhood. The east side frames a shaded urban plaza shared by students and the public. The north side opens onto

"As a public institution, Portland State University has a responsibility for public service and stewardship. This responsibility extends to the students we teach, the community we serve and the land we inhabit."

—"SUSTAINABILITY At Portland State University: A Self-Guided Tour", 2006

a pedestrian plaza with large oversized windows that let in as much light as possible. The south façade, towards the interstate, utilizes smaller windows and built-in solar shades to minimize sun exposure.

Additional design features were included to alter the building's overall reliance on mechanical and electrical systems and dramatically reduce resource consumption well beyond code requirements. These are: high performance glazing, maximum daylighting, and exterior sunshades on the south and west elevations. Also, the building's floor plan accommodates natural cross- and stack-ventilation. Operable windows remove heat and provide cooling and daylight to more than 98 percent of internal spaces. Waste heat recovery from mechanical and electrical systems assists in pre-heating air.

Above all, Epler Hall's most distinctive feature is its innovative stormwater management scheme. Portland's plentiful rain flows from the rooftop through downspouts to river rock splash boxes, then through "rainwater runnels" across the plaza and into planter boxes. There, water is aerated before entering an underground storage tank for reuse in toilets and on-site irrigation.

INTEGRATED DESIGN PROCESS

During early stages of planning in 2001, PSU administration, the Facilities Management Department and the property manager, College Housing Northwest, expressed their common interest in demonstration student housing and a classroom to showcase the university's Sustainability Program. The group also declared its commitment to be the first USGBC LEED® project on campus as well as the first mixed-use LEED® building in Portland.

To accomplish these goals, the university selected Mithun, Walsh Construction Company and Interface Engineering based on their combined experience with sustainable design and LEED. The project team added sustainability expertise early in the design phase with Portland-based Green Building Services Inc. and the Northwest Energy Efficiency Alliance's BetterBricks Program. Additionally, city representatives and PSU students were vital to the decision-making process.

The Oregon Department of Energy also contributed to the project through the State Energy Efficiency Design Program. This program requires energy review of all new state university-owned buildings and major renovations to ensure that cost-effective energy measures are included and that energy efficiency is at least 20 percent higher than code.

THE SITE

On what was once the location of the old thirteen-unit Birmingham Housing building in the University District's student housing neighborhood now stands Epler Hall at SW 12th Avenue and Montgomery Street. It is one of more than fifty PSU academic, residential, administrative, office and recreational buildings in Portland's urban downtown center.

Bordered by the PSU campus to the east and north, and on the south and west by Interstate 405, the site is close to multiple transit opportunities including bus, light rail and streetcars. The building is oriented north-south to preserve large, existing trees and maximize its adaptability within the campus master plan.

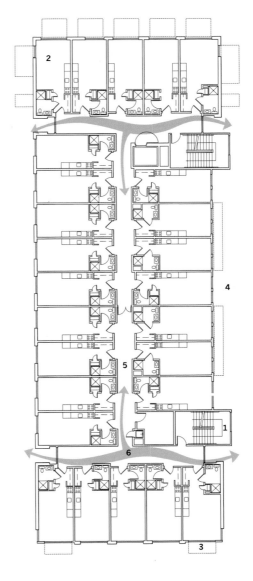

FLOORPLAN: Five of the building's six stories feature small Euro-style studio units, so efficient that excess heat from lights and a computer monitor is enough to warm each room during most of the year. Throughout Epler Hall are a combination of passive design measures, the corridors naturally cross-ventilated and cooled with operable windows at each end.

1 oversized stair to encourage pedestrian travel
2 windows correspond to solar orientation
3 sunshades on south & west elevations
4 operable windows (typ)
5 natural ventilation shafts
6 thru ventilation

0'　　　　　40'　　　N

THE WATER STORY: Epler Hall's rainwater harvesting system is built into the landscape and makes for an engaging street-level display during storms: water shoots down a five-story downspout and out into a rock-filled basin, then directed into a runnel and across the plaza, finally flowing to underground retention tanks for treatment using UV light and held for re-use.

The west side of Epler Hall fronts an urban sidewalk, while the east side faces a shaded plaza with covered seating. The plaza is shielded from highway noise and the western sun – providing cool, fresh air for the building. Previously, this location was the site of a service station. Today, in place of the buried storage tanks and contaminated soils, which had to be removed, are bio-swales and grounds covered in drought-tolerant plantings.

THE PROGRAM
The six-story residence hall includes one hundred-thirty studio units for students, situated over ground-level classrooms and faculty offices. Each 280-square-foot apartment has window openings sized relative to their solar orientation and natural ventilation needs. Corridors are naturally cross-ventilated with operable windows at each end.

Epler Hall's ground floor is home to the university's Center for Science Education; the top floor hosts a "Global Village" residence life program pairing international and local students. Wide stairways between each floor are designed to encourage student interaction.

Parking is located underground to preserve open space. Individual bike storage has been included within each apartment and on the first level to encourage use of alternate transportation. Likewise, shower facilities, changing areas and a bicycle cleaning station are included for biking commuters. A new recycling center adjacent to the site serves Epler Hall as well as other nearby residence halls.

STRUCTURE & MATERIALS
Demolition of the old Birmingham afforded several recycling

opportunities, including the salvage of 90 percent of the brick and re-use of many fixtures for the new building. Mithun's specifications for the studio apartments also emphasized regionally-produced and renewable materials such as engineered lumber products. Interior door trim is made from MDF; counter cores are pine with 100 percent recycled fiber; cabinet cores are made from wheatboard; and interior door cores are made with composite material. The carpet is CRI green label.

On the exterior, the roof is four-ply modified bitumen with heat-reflecting elastomeric coating. The building envelope is comprised of twelve-inch-wide flat seam metal wall panels with 12 to 15 percent recycled content. In addition, custom fabricated sunshades contain 80 percent recycled steel (post consumer or post industrial).

ENERGY
The combination of ultra-efficient design techniques and Energy Star appliances employed for the student residences has resulted in a 35 percent reduction of total energy usage versus the 2001 Oregon Energy Code. Individually, the studio apartments are designed to be so efficient they can be heated by a student's computer and unit lighting on all but the coldest days, although electric baseboards are provided as a backup.

HEATING & COOLING
A sunlight model of the building was developed during the project's early design phases. Created by the Northwest Energy Efficiency Alliance, this model aided Mithun's designers in determining optimum size and placement of exterior sunshades on the west

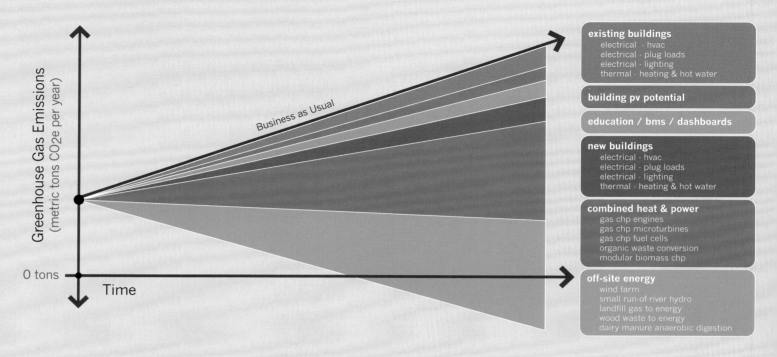

ENERGY-RELATED GREENHOUSE GAS REDUCTION STRATEGIES

The chart shows:
- Greenhouse Gas Emissions (metric tons CO2e per year) on vertical axis
- Time on horizontal axis
- Business as Usual trend line
- 0 tons baseline

Categories listed on right:
- **existing buildings** — electrical · hvac / electrical · plug loads / electrical · lighting / thermal · heating & hot water
- **building pv potential**
- **education / bms / dashboards**
- **new buildings** — electrical · hvac / electrical · plug loads / electrical · lighting / thermal · heating & hot water
- **combined heat & power** — gas chp engines / gas chp microturbines / gas chp fuel cells / organic waste conversion / modular biomass chp
- **off-site energy** — wind farm / small run-of-river hydro / landfill gas to energy / wood waste to energy / dairy manure anaerobic digestion

SEATTLE UNIVERSITY:
"Aiming high, to be a carbon-neutral campus"

Seattle University's (SU) tradition of sustainability dates back more than two decades. An early supporter of the American College and University Presidents Climate Commitment, the university has earned accolades for its innovative landscape practices, purchase of renewable energy and other environmental initiatives. So it came as no surprise when SU asked Mithun to lead development of a master plan coupled with a Sustainable Master Plan designed to set comprehensive goals for carbon emissions, energy use and water use reductions on a scale never attempted before. Located at the edge of Seattle's central business district, SU has grown to thirty buildings on forty-eight acres. The plan's driving force is the "Triple Top Line" of planet, people and prosperity – an emphasis not just on energy, water and carbon but also on establishing meaningful metrics for "people systems."

The Princeton Wedge – part of Mithun's portfolio of tools used to help the university fulfill its mission to be carbon neutral as the campus grows. Together, Mithun and campus planners are exploring the idea of a "stabilization triangle", itself divided into a series of "wedges" (efficiency, carbon capture, solar) that would each reduce a portion of carbon emissions. Dozens of strategies then combine within these wedges to cut emissions powerfully over time: from demand reduction and combined heat and power to rainwater reuse, high performance landscapes, restored native habitats and more – all focused on human well-being, vital ecological systems, a healthy university.

"There is no precedent for a campus sustainable master plan as integrated and comprehensive as this one. A lot of universities are addressing sustainability but that usually involves a whole range of initiatives happening in different places across campus. In terms of a workable tool, we think Seattle U's plan is going to take higher education sustainability to the next level."

—*Brodie Bain, AIA, Mithun*

Seattle University, Seattle, Washington

Housing Master Plan, completed June 2008

Supports the university's goal of a 60 percent residential population over the next twenty years; creating an "integrated learning environment" focused on residence halls where the students live and learn

Major Institution Master Plan (MIMP), completed June 2008

Applies city codes and process and guides the future development of campus as it relates to the surrounding community; directs massing, setbacks, heights limits and zoning issues

Sustainable Master Plan, to be completed Summer 2009

Examines climate goals, energy resource flow, water resource flow, ecosystem services and habitat quality of land cover, as well as a full range of carbon, energy and water use strategies: building efficiencies, PV, on- and off-site energy reduction, landscape practices such as soil rebuilding, carbon storage, composting, integrated test management, invasives management, rainwater reuse, reduced impervious surfaces

SOUTH SEATTLE COMMUNITY COLLEGE: "Discovering a new campus center"

South Seattle Community College (SCCC) is in a state of transition: emerging as a new kind of institution, innovating, one of the state's first two-year colleges to add four-year degrees to its broad mix of vocational and technical programs. Located on an eighty seven-acre hilltop in residential West Seattle, the college serves nearly eight thousand students enrolled in workforce and worker retaining programs such as aviation, culinary arts, health care and horticulture, as well as academic transfer programs and opportunities to earn a bachelor's degree through partner institutions. Over time, the circa 1970s office park-style campus had expanded without any clear sense of order or structure. So Mithun's challenge in 2003 was to create a new center for SCCC by enhancing its existing open space and concentrating public functions. The resulting master plan successfully links the school's technical and

academic zones, while strengthening the sense of community on campus and increasing connections to surrounding neighborhoods.

The University Center then becomes the first element of a new campus center, also forming the edge of its new academic green. Home to university partners, classrooms and faculty offices, the building features a floor-to-ceiling glass wall and two-story atrium from which occupants can look out over this open space. Conversely, the design invites passers-by to look inside, through the transparent façade, where fellow students are pursuing four-year degrees. Daylit and naturally ventilated, the Center reinforces the master plan's concept to create a visible, welcoming place for campus and community with a clear vision to the future.

South Seattle Community College, West Seattle, Washington

University Center, two-story, 15,000 square feet, completed September 2006

Durable, low-maintenance structural concrete shell, daylighting, natural ventilation, bioswales for water filtration, rain garden

AIA Seattle Project of the Month, October 2007

Campus Master Plan, 87 acres, completed 2007

Reduces vehicle miles traveled to campus, parking requirements, decreases amount of impervious surfaces, maintains green corridor surrounding campus

"The new University Center was inspired by three related design concepts: the Beacon, the Edge and the Zipper. Like a beacon, it is open, glowing, attracting and orienting students as the new academic center of campus. By forming a strong edge, it defines the new quadrangle. And like a zipper, it brings together both the technical and academic parts of the college."

—*Ron van der Veen, AIA, Mithun*

"Stephen Epler left a legacy that is the cornerstone of what Portland State University is about: service to the community and responsiveness to the region."

—*PSU President Daniel O. Bernstine*

and south façades. The sunshades effectively delay heat gain from sunlight – cooling the building during summer months while maximizing views and natural lighting.

No cooling systems were installed upstairs. The top five floors of Epler Hall utilize natural cross-ventilation in the corridors during the summer, while a heat-exchange wheel recovers lost heat from building exhaust in winter. Along with night cooling of the building mass, the first floor relies primarily on incoming air from operable windows along the perimeter, combined with a "solar chimney" designed to draw hot air out of the top of the building and achieve a comfortable indoor environment. This "stack effect" features five 50-foot tall shafts that extend to the roof.

LIGHTING & DAYLIGHTING
Epler Hall was designed to use as much natural light as possible. The studio units on the west side of the building feature floor-to-ceiling windows. They were the first to be rented. Lighting is further managed with occupancy sensors in the classrooms and daylighting controls in the stairwells and corridors.

INDOOR AIR
To support the building's overall emphasis on indoor air quality, every efficiency studio was finished with low-emitting VOC paints and glues and formaldehyde-free materials. Units were designed with window openings sized relative to their solar orientation and ventilation needs. The corridors of each floor naturally cross ventilate with operable windows – essentially, "gills" – at each end.

The first-floor offices and classrooms feature operable windows and mechanically-assisted natural ventilation shafts.

WATER
The building's architecture also tells an important story of natural resources and recycling, of openly expressing the movement of water in its urban context. Epler's rainwater harvesting system is designed to be interactive and interesting to the public, demonstrating the creative, environmentally-friendly options possible in sustainable design. Rain on the rooftops of Epler Hall and adjacent King Albert Hall is diverted into visible collection areas and then flows down to river rock splash boxes within the public plaza where students gather.

In addition to stormwater catchment, many facets of the mechanical and plumbing system designs are geared toward energy efficiency. Project engineers specified low-flow plumbing fixtures on the ground floor and in all apartment units, fixtures that use 10 percent less water than the existing low-flow standard. These combined strategies make it possible for the building to reduce its water consumption by more than 30 percent versus a conventional residence hall.

Epler Hall also demonstrates the larger city-wide advantage conferred by PSU's investment in sustainable design. As water resources become more strained, and municipal infrastructure costs escalate, reduced demand on the Portland water supply will have a significant external impact. In turn, an analysis one year after completion of the residence hall showed the economic benefit to Portland State: a joint 14 percent ROI for energy and water without the city's stormwater rebate, and a joint 19 percent ROI with the rebate.

SMART STRUCTURE: In addition to its innovative
stormwater management scheme, the building's
climate-responsive design greatly reduces reliance
on mechanical and electrical systems. The floor
plan of the six-story residence hall also aids
natural cross- and stack-ventilation.

1 water detention filtered for reuse in irrigation
  and flushing first floor toilets
2 bioswale
3 courtyard plaza
4 rainwater collection
5 natural ventilation
6 studios
7 classrooms

EPLER'S POST OCCUPANCY

The proof is in the walls, windows, roof – and water efficiency of Stephen Epler Hall. Just one year after it was completed, achieving status as a LEED® Silver project, a PSU Environmental Management Master's student conducted a landmark study of the building's water and energy savings. In her Final Report[2] of March 2005, Cathy Turner's financial analysis concluded:

> "If savings from lower water and energy usage continue at their initial levels, they will generate a return on that investment worth over $700,000 and generate an average return of approximately 14 percent."

This saving was the return achieved by Epler Hall for the academic year 2003-2004, based on resource costs for that year and as analyzed in 2005. During its first year of operation, energy use at Epler Hall is approximately 49 percent less than code, with a 17 percent ROI. These findings are especially important considering how energy costs have escalated since the fall of 2004, so that ROI can be extrapolated to serve as an economic model in response to changing energy and water costs.

The study, A First Year Evaluation of the Energy and Water Conservation of Epler Hall, addresses three questions regarding the efficiency and conservation features of the six-story residence hall:

1. Is the building achieving the anticipated energy and water efficiency?
2. What are PSU's direct savings from these efficiency features?
3. Does the conservation generate additional societal benefits, beyond the direct PSU savings?

Turner also notes: "The design and construction costs for Epler Hall totaled $10 million (in 2003). That included a net investment in water and energy conservation features, after receipt of various conservation grants and incentive payments, of about $290,000."

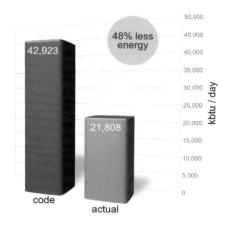

PER CAPITA ENERGY USE

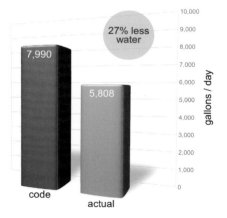

DAILY POTABLE WATER USE

PSU EPLER HALL ANNUAL DIRECT SAVINGS

	INCREMENTAL INITIAL COSTS	ANNUAL SAVINGS	25 YEAR PRESENT VALUE[1]	RETURN ON INVESTMENT	BREAK EVEN YEAR
ENERGY	$200,000	$34,000	$600,000	17%	7
WATER, SEWER, AND STORMWATER	$90,000	$7,000	$120,000	5%	18
TOTAL	$290,000	$41,000	$720,000	14%	9

[1] "A present value represents the value today of payments to be received in the future. The present values in this table assume a real discount rate of 3 percent/year, which the National Institute of Standards specifies for long term life cycle costing of federal energy calculations. That means that, in the absence of inflation, the certainty of receiving $1 one year from now would have the same value as having $0.97 today. "

She adds that a rebate received from the City of Portland for stormwater reduction strategies would raise the water ROI to much higher levels: "Epler Hall's demonstrated first-year savings in water use allowed PSU to obtain a reduction of $79,000 in the system development fees levied by the city on new construction. Similar arrangements may not be negotiable on future new buildings (at PSU,) so this saving is not included in the table. However, for Epler Hall, this fee reduction will more than cover all the initial costs of the water conservation features." With the rebate included, the ROI becomes much more significant at 19 percent.

PSU EPLER HALL ANNUAL DIRECT SAVINGS WITH WATER REBATE

	INCREMENTAL INITIAL COSTS	ANNUAL SAVINGS	25 YEAR PRESENT VALUE[1]	RETURN ON INVESTMENT	BREAK EVEN YEAR
ENERGY	$200,000	$34,000	$600,000	17%	7
WATER, SEWER, AND STORMWATER	$11,000	$7,000	$125,000	64%	2
TOTAL	$211,000	$41,000	$725,000	19%	6

LIVING/LEARNING: High performance glazing, maximum daylighting, exterior sunshades on the south and west elevations – all combine at Epler Hall to create a high quality environment for students. In addition, operable windows provide cooling and daylight to more than 98 percent of internal spaces.

PRINCIPLE 5

DO THE MATH

ULI REALITY CHECK

''The Seattle Reality Check was uniquely and totally congruent with Mithun's values. There was no better vehicle for us to continue to promote what we feel are the critical issues and goals of responsible, sustainable growth in the region. This was not just a great think-tank exercise; it has implementation wheels, it will roll.''

—William Kreager, FAIA, Mithun, Co-Chair of Reality Check 2008

ULI REALITY CHECK

Seattle, Washington

April 30, 2008

"We have work to do"

They came to brainstorm, to analyze – to imagine a future Seattle. On this spring day, hundreds of political, business, community and environmental leaders were invited to the University of Washington. Their purpose: a participatory, GIS-based exercise to develop alternative growth scenarios for the four-county metropolitan area, expected to absorb 1.7 million people by the year 2040. Sponsored by the Urban Land Institute (ULI), Reality Check was also the first-ever workshop to focus on comprehensive housing/transportation/growth/ carbon challenges for the Puget Sound region. Mithun joined ULI Seattle and the Puget Sound Regional Council as major sponsors.

So the "game" was set: at each of the thirty-two tables, a diverse group of stakeholders and policy leaders – "players" – laid out a distinct vision of community. Colored LEGOs and yarn were placed on maps of the region to represent projected households, jobs and transportation options. Mithun staff volunteered to calculate each team's carbon footprint and further illustrate how these planning approaches might achieve their goals of carbon neutrality. What follows is a two-year implementation process funded by ULI to support the region through educational forums, technical assistance and an awards program recognizing the best in smart growth.

Is it possible to measure the value of fresh air and sunshine? Or calculate the benefits of rainwater? Or put a price tag on protecting a century-old Douglas Fir in the midst of a new housing development? "Do the Math" increasingly guides the work of Mithun through inquiry, testing and analysis, a practice of quantifying and qualifying ideas – with every concept, every design decision, every planning matrix. That discipline still resonates in researching material choices: which interior finish is healthier, which wood windows are FSC certified. Using reviews of local culture and history to inform the re-design of urban neighborhoods. Discovering new tools to assess embodied energy or the lifecycle costs of a project even before it is built.

If you have the question and there is no answer, the most important step is to ask the question – because somebody will figure out the answer.

Focusing on the facts means goal setting with metrics, a consistent rigor in specifications. Merging spirit and economics. Seizing every opportunity to further the science through design.

It is a process of discovery that blurs the lines between developer and designer, vendor, consultant and regulator. Breaking down silos. A collective willingness to risk. Collaborating with the public and with competitors: to ask, solve and interact with still more ideas. Mithun's math was critical in the post-occupancy evaluation of a new university dormitory, demonstrating impressive ROI in the face of mounting water and energy costs. And with the development of an online carbon calculator, this new tool holds promise in using the power of the market to create change.

CHAPTER 7:
MITHUN OFFICES, PIER 56

INTRODUCTION

RENEWING THE WATERFRONT

"...Yes, there is still the sea. It laps the barnacled piers, oily and salty, and warm with the color of the sunset blazing behind the Olympic Mountains as they define the western sky in serene and snowy beauty."
Nancy Wilson Ross, Farthest Reach

"As we thought about the kind of place we wanted to be, what kind of statement we wanted to make about Mithun's work...Pier 56 afforded us a unique opportunity. So we made a conscious decision to engage our neighborhood, the city and the whole waterfront in a positive way."

—*Thom Emrich, AIA, Mithun*

Once, the piers along the Seattle waterfront would stretch as far as the eye could see: jutting out into Elliott Bay, connecting the rapidly-growing city to Puget Sound and finally, the Pacific Ocean.

Built in 1900, Pier 56 was one of three large waterfront supply terminals erected by the Northern Pacific Railroad to support the Klondike Gold Rush and Pacific trade. During the golden age of Seattle's maritime commerce, the piers were fixtures in the booming steamship business along the Northwest coast. And when the Port of Seattle began its shift to containerized cargo after World War II, the piers found renewed life as home to seafood restaurants, import stores and other tourist attractions.

In April 2000 Mithun became the newest tenant of Pier 56, relocating its offices into the entire second floor of this historic site.

MITHUN OFFICES, PIER 56
Seattle, Washington

That conscious decision was significant for Mithun in several ways. The practice was growing but committed to staying in downtown Seattle. Mithun's leadership also wanted office space that was distinctive, historic, something that embodied the evolving culture and goals of the firm.

Choices were limited with the building stock available downtown. So the idea of inhabiting a vacant pier warehouse on the waterfront emerged as an intriguing option. By conducting interior tenant improvements simultaneously with work on the exterior envelope, the entire Pier 56 redevelopment was completed within a significantly compressed schedule.

The building renovation also came to signify community and connection. In selecting this site, Mithun knew the office would create year-round activity in what is primarily a seasonal tourist area and contribute to the vitality of the neighborhood. Most importantly, the decision to occupy Pier 56 allowed Mithun to demonstrate its commitment to sustainable design. The open, 27,340-square-foot space is exemplary in its use of environmentally-friendly materials, recycled content, energy efficiency, and natural cooling. It provides abundant daylight, fresh air and public spaces that allow all staff and visitors to experience the history and natural environment of the waterfront.

DESIGN OVERVIEW
In bringing Pier 56 back to life, Mithun wanted to establish a contemporary design with its new office while restoring the building's original structural elements. All interior surfaces of the original timber structure were sandblasted and left exposed to highlight the building's distinctive turn-of-the-century materials. Clerestory windows on the south and north sides respect the scale and proportion of the pier's historical character.

The primary design goal for Pier 56 was to create an open office environment for employees, clients and visitors – and further emphasize the linear spatial experience of the original warehouse. Preserving this open space would achieve the project's design themes of

POINT NO POINT: It is known as "Point No Point" in Mithun's office: a common space for impromptu meetings, staff parties, guest lectures, exhibits, and many functions open to the public – with spectacular views over Elliott Bay to the Olympic Mountains in the west.

HISTORY MAKING: Pier 56 was the site where President Theodore Roosevelt disembarked on May 23, 1903 during his visit to the city – greeted by one of the largest crowds ever to assemble in Seattle.

PIERS ON THE WATERFRONT, 1933: Constructed to support Pacific shipping in another era, the piers came to define and energize the city's rapid growth through World War II. Today, after many efforts by the Port of Seattle to modernize the waterfront, most of the pier buildings are gone.

flexibility, collaboration and egalitarianism. As a first step, many interior walls were removed, leaving only those necessary for seismic upgrades to the building or for spaces requiring special acoustic or light control.

To complement this openness, designers also included autonomous "vessels" for required private spaces such as conference rooms. These vessels are closed forms, the space inside distinct from the surrounding area and each oriented off the grid of the existing structure. Walls are painted in rich colors to contrast with the dominant wood columns, trusses, ceiling joists and decking. Shear walls were placed where they would be least disruptive. One distinct vessel frames the edge of the lobby where the entry area functions as a transition between the quiet office space and busy tourist attractions outside.

Another fundamental goal was to create project-oriented workspaces. By definition, this layout would support the continuous formation of project teams, impromptu mentoring, and expertise sharing across market areas within the firm. Mithun envisioned the office as a non-hierarchical working environment, encouraging active participation among all design and support staff, rather than organizing the space around individual designers or studios.

Opening up the office has also supported the firm's belief in design as a public process. Essential to this idea are common areas distributed throughout the building. In particular, "Main Street" runs down the middle of the office and serves as a linear public venue to encourage broader interaction among colleagues and collaborators. Visitors, too, may venture beyond the reception area to view the

firm's work and experience all aspects of the design process. At the far end of the pier, a large open space known as "Point No Point" invites public gatherings with expansive floor-to-ceiling windows that frame quintessential Seattle views such as harbor activity, commuter ferry boats and the Olympic Mountains.

INTEGRATED DESIGN PROCESS

The Pier 56 renovation depended on a unique set of partnerships between the developer, Martin Smith Inc., Mithun's board of directors, the tenant's design team (Mithun), the architect responsible for exterior envelope improvements (Daly & Associates), the shell and core contractor (J.R. Abbott Construction), and a second contractor for tenant improvements (Edifice Construction). This complex team participated in a series of strategy and visioning meetings to ensure that Mithun's new office space met the needs of all key stakeholders.

Initial redevelopment of Pier 56 had begun in the 1990s, but never followed a clear goal. Until Mithun chose to relocate here, the building was a windowless warehouse requiring significant improvements even to function as raw office space. Only the eastern end of the building facing Alaskan Way was in use by Elliott's Oyster House and a few other retail spaces. For Mithun, the TI design team identified several strategies for an open layout that would incorporate reclaimed and sustainable materials and minimize costs. The owner's original redevelopment plans did not call for natural ventilation; but Mithun made a convincing case, including a budget analysis, to increase glazing and introduce energy-efficient heating. A fluid dynamic model further demonstrated the viability of a passively-cooled building.

LONG LIFE, LOOSE FIT: Flexibility was a primary goal of tenant improvements in restoring the old warehouse: to create an environment of open work areas and still retain the aura of the existing structure, while taking advantage of the waterfront's cooling breezes.

By necessity, this fast track project (beginning summer 1999) required a strong working relationship between the two architecture firms. Mithun also served as a consultant to Daly & Associates on the shell's re-design and relocation of the lobby, as well as the fenestration, canopies and balconies on the exterior. The two contractors had to coordinate their efforts closely, working under difficult winter construction conditions to complete the work in less than five months.

THE SITE
Seattle's historic urban waterfront forms one of the largest tourist-oriented areas of the city, vibrant and alive with harbor cruise boats, restaurants, ice cream and souvenir shops. Pier 56 is bordered on the south by a Washington State ferry terminal and on the north by the Seattle Aquarium. An elevated expressway stands between the pier and downtown.

Renovation of this existing structure built over water brought its own set of challenges for the project team. The team's first task was to tie the whole building together and make it seismically sound – especially difficult because the building was ten inches out of plumb at the west end, the consequence of a ship collision in the 1940s. These predominantly timber pier structures require very different connections than what is common with land-based construction processes.

QUIET SPACE: Even with more than two hundred people spread over an open floor plan, the office is relatively quiet. Mithun retained an acoustic consultant to work with the design team on minimizing noise levels. Essentially, the same fans bringing in fresh air from outside generate "white" background noise to successfully mask even the sound of a busy expressway nearby.

THE PROGRAM
The entryway to Mithun's office is a separate form, containing only a stair and elevator and emerging directly into the old second-story warehouse. Today, the linear space is characterized by a high central

bay with clerestory windows and equal side bays on each side, oriented with views back to the city on the east end and views across Elliott Bay to the Olympic Mountains in the west. The program called for three-quarters of the area, with the remainder available for a subtenant and future growth.

Further into the office are the open, project-centric work areas, featuring a series of long singular tables. Each workstation at the tables can expand or contract as project teams grow or shrink throughout design and construction. To facilitate collaboration and flexibility, individuals can easily move from one work table to another. Additional custom-built "project islands" between the tables create a central location for drawings, files and other material storage, as well as team meetings.

Public spaces throughout the office are vitally important to Mithun's culture and work processes. "Main Street" is oversized to allow for crits, displays, informal meetings, and employee encounters. Larger public spaces are located at the western end, while production, resources and an open model shop are concentrated near the center.

STRUCTURE & MATERIALS

After more than a century of use, the integrity of the structure was considered sound and required very little reconstruction. Project carpenters were particularly impressed with the engineering of the entire truss and floor system.

Mithun's deliberate emphasis on reused, recycled and post-production waste products, as well as locally-available materials,

BIOPHILIA:
"Splendor awaits in minute proportions"[1]

It is a clearing in the forest. A view to the bay. The feel of warm daylight or a cool breeze, spaces defined by raw, honest materials, a sense of movement, of change over time. Mithun's designs have long been influenced by the ideas of biophilia ("love of life and the living world") – from its Everwood offices through REI's Seattle and Denver flagships, to IslandWood, Epler Hall, Zoomazium and many more. Today, the drive to more fully embrace biophilia continues – to create places that evoke nature's patterns; landscapes and interiors that teach or bring perspective, joy and comfort. To that end, Mithun has adopted seven attributes that serve as the basis of its design approach practice-wide: "Sensory Richness"; "Motion"; "Serendipity"; "Variations on a Theme"; "Resilience"; "Sense of Freeness"; and "Prospect, Refuge and Enticement". Further explorations by Mithun continue, as well, through research and collaboration with the University of Washington and elsewhere – seeking new ways to incorporate natural elements into its designs.

"A rich sensory environment surrounds us, not just with visual delight, but also with sounds, haptic sensations from the feel of wood or stone, and variations in temperature and light as we move through a space."[2] Mithun's expression of biophilic design is increasingly clear in projects such as Novelty Hill-Januik Winery, the new Telemedicine Center at UC Irvine, and especially throughout its own Pier 56 office: quiet, colorful, open, places of prospect and refuge.

Biophilia

bio•phil•ia, noun, 1979 : a hypothetical human tendency to
interact or be closely associated with other forms of life in nature

Greenbuild 2006: "Biophilic Design: Principles, Practices and
Benefits"

Led by: Stephen Kellert, Yale University; Judith Heerwagen, J.H.
Heerwagen & Associates, Inc.; Bert Gregory, Mithun; Amelia
Floresta, Kieran Timberlake Associates; Jonathan Rose, Jonathan
Rose Companies LLC

Biophilic Design, "Biophilia and Sensory Aesthetics", Judith
Heerwagen, Ph.D. and Bert Gregory, FAIA

"How can we take advantage of natural systems to create
environments that are more beneficial to people's well-being, or that
protect and even restore the natural features of a site? Thinking of
biophilia, of our innate connection to nature, helps us create places
that people are going to love, that will be more resilient in the long
term."

—*Critter Thompson, Systems Ecologist, Mithun*

is evident throughout the space. Reclaimed timbers were used in the new lobby entry area as stair treads and structural decking on the stairwell. Mezzanines – included for future growth – were constructed of parallel strand beams made from post-production waste material. Sisal floor covering in conference rooms is made from 100 percent biodegradable natural fiber, while carpet tiles in work areas contain 98 percent recycled content. The kitchen floor is a mosaic of ceramic tile and stone samples recycled from the firm's old product library. And particle board floor panels (OSB), made of post-production waste materials, are featured along Main Street and in the large public area at the pier's west end.

Additionally, workstations were constructed of strawboard panels, with formaldehyde-free, pre-finished plywood used for shelving units. Natural plywood surfaces at the clerestory were substituted for painted drywall.

ENERGY

Mithun's Pier 56 office reduces energy consumption dramatically through a variety of strategies and revisions to the owner's original plans. Chief among these is reliance on passive cooling and the installation of operable windows for natural ventilation. Double-glazed, insulated windows also maximize window efficiency and minimize thermal bridging. The roof was upgraded from R-21 to R-30 insulation.

HEATING & COOLING

Its high, open ceilings and waterfront location makes passive cooling

ideal for Pier 56. Natural ventilation modeling conducted by KEEN Engineering in the design phase gave building owners the confidence to move ahead without mechanical air conditioning. Mithun also convinced them to minimize ductwork within the space and simplify the HVAC scheme with a high-efficiency boiler and fan coil unit system to supply heat in winter and assist air circulation in summer.

Because the office space is essentially one large volume, Mithun developed an operations strategy that relies on operable windows to manage prevailing airflows and maximize cooling effects. Clerestories and perimeter windows are operated by staff, using cranks distributed throughout the space. The design team kept enclosed rooms to a minimum and placed circulation at the perimeter. Several comfort zones exist within the space at any one time, with temperatures varying six to eight degrees depending on the time of day and location within the building. Also, the south- and west-facing windows feature sunshading devices, while north-facing windows are open to maximize natural lighting.

LIGHTING & DAYLIGHTING

Mithun's office design provides for high levels of daylighting year round. North-facing windows were arranged to maximize available lighting. The increase in overall glazing areas and the specially-designed operable windows take full advantage of natural light, reducing the need for electric lighting during the day. A programmable low-voltage control system automatically controls light fixtures in all areas of the office.

PRIME WORKPLACE: Pier 56 has become one of the most enviable places to work in all of Seattle – its renovation successfully balancing sustainable design with the inherent beauty of a historic structure. Mechanical and electrical systems minimize energy consumption by avoiding air conditioning and providing 85 percent of the lighting allowed by the energy code.

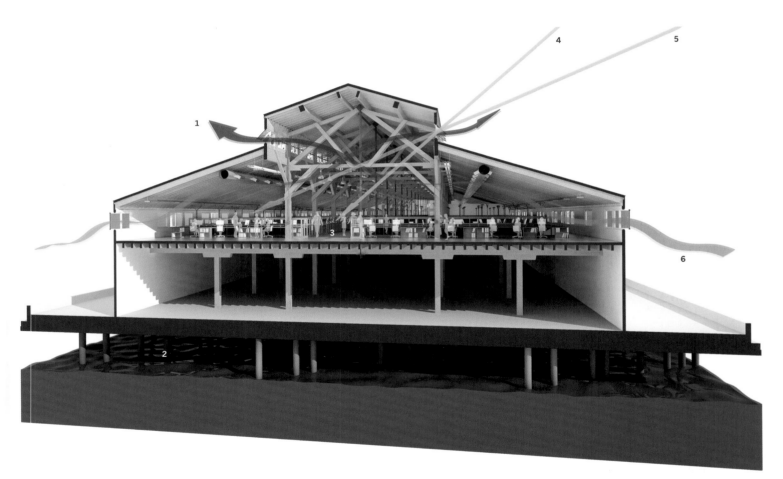

1 heat ventilates through clerestory windows
2 Pier 56, Seattle
3 open office plan
4 summer sun
5 winter sun
6 cross-ventilation and natural cooling through
   operable side windows

FLOORPLAN: Mithun's offices fill the second floor of this heavy timber structure, which totals 100 feet wide and nearly 400 feet long, the open work areas patterned on a system of flexible work spines allowing staff to reorganize easily. The design reflects the use of "vessels" throughout the interior space, including the entryway and five semi-enclosed conference rooms.

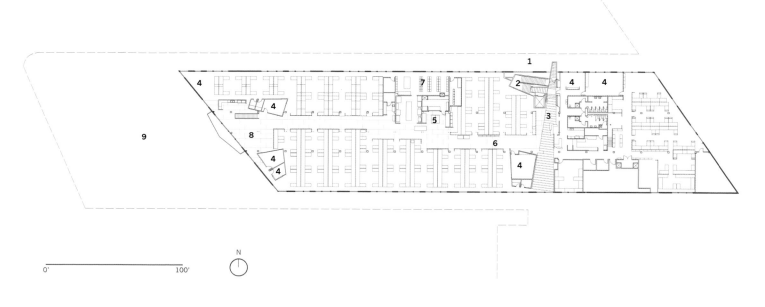

1 entry
2 stair
3 reception
4 conference room
5 model shop
6 Main Street
7 materials library
8 Point No Point
9 pier parking

Beautiful view to the Olympic Mountains from
Point No Point

INDOOR AIR

The open layout and operable windows provide fresh air and breezes from Puget Sound for the entire office. Seattle city code also required the use of two large fan units to move fresh air. Located unobtrusively under the clerestory, the fans exhaust circulated air at the west and east ends of the space. To promote effective use of this natural ventilation scheme, KEEN supplied an occupant's guidebook to explain different seasonal demands on the space.

Special care was also given to indoor environmental quality. Low-VOC paints and sealers and water-based urethane finishes were used on all walls and desktops; flooring materials were applied with low-toxicity glues.

WATER

To minimize water consumption, the office has low-flow toilets, water-efficient dishwashers and waterless urinals installed in the men's room.

ACCESS

Important to Mithun's overall sustainability goals, the Pier 56 location also offers employees several mass transit options. The office is just two blocks from the ferry terminal, one block from a waterfront trolley and three blocks from a major regional transit hub. The design also included showers and lockers to encourage individuals to bike or run to work.

PIER 56: YOU ARE HERE

Pier 56 has a rich and varied history as part of Seattle's central waterfront:

This pier was "The Gateway to Alaska" for gold seekers on their way to Canada's Klondike Gold Rush.

President Theodore Roosevelt disembarked here during his May 23, 1903 visit to Seattle and was greeted by one of the largest crowds ever to assemble in the city.

In the early part of the 20th century, Frank Waterhouse was a big name on the waterfront: his steamships were the first to regularly reach the Mediterranean from Puget Sound.

During the 1960s, Pier 56 was home to the Seattle Marine Aquarium and its contentious display of captured killer whales (orcas), beginning with the famous Namu.

HAND HEWN: The pier's interior emphasizes raw, honest materials throughout the 36,000-square-foot space – the heavy timber trusses originally hand hewn at a 45 degree angle. For the renovation, all surfaces were blasted with copper slag, a post-industrial waste product, to expose the connections and natural wood surfaces.

PRINCIPLE 6

STRENGTHEN COMMUNITY

YESLER COMMUNITY CENTER

"Here, the spaces between are as important as the primary program elements. Cranking apart some of those elements resulted in open space that enhances community, that creates a internal sidewalk or street running through the middle of the building to connect with the neighborhood."

—Rich Franko, AIA, Mithun

YESLER COMMUNITY CENTER

Seattle, Washington

February 2005

"Bringing the city through the building"

This is a place of belonging, a place for people within this international neighborhood in Seattle's First Hill district that overlooks downtown. From its entrance along Yesler Way and throughout the center's varied spaces, the modern architecture is rich and warm. The scale, materials and sequence of the exterior complement those of the interior. Most importantly, the design of this new multi-story, 30,000-square-foot building just feels good, cheerful, safe: full of spaces to interact naturally, to build community.

Operated by Seattle Parks and Recreation, the center serves Yesler

Terrace, a racially-diverse, low-income community of fifteen hundred residents who collectively speak nine different languages. Mithun's thoughtful design reflects the building's many uses. The long, open Reception/Lobby area is welcoming – full of color, art, photography – and oriented to monitor all comings and goings. In addition to the large Multipurpose Room, a series of activity spaces are located throughout. Yesler's Gymnasium is flooded with light, full of fresh air. Operable windows and skylights enhance natural cooling and ventilation – here and everywhere. Informed further by its energy and water savings and use of recycled materials, this LEED® Gold center defines community: bright, family friendly, a place for gathering, and sustainable.

INTEGRATED DESIGN: MITHUN

Community is shared experience and memory. Collective wisdom. Building trust, building relationships that last. Mithun's call to "Strengthen Community" is clear and conscious, a reminder to include the human element in design – to not forget about people – when challenged with environmental, technical or zoning issues. That means creating a new public space for employees of one company, a space that becomes the heart and soul of its corporate campus. Of reinforcing a neighborhood's connectedness, from every front porch to its sidewalks, streets and open spaces and to the larger community beyond. And understanding the importance of gathering places, of form and symbol, ritual and nature for a tribal master plan.

Community implies responsibility: to the people who will inhabit it, to those who will pass by, those who will use it in the future, even those who are not born yet – and to other species.

Being a good neighbor. Citizenship. Respect. Joint ownership, finding common ground. It is Main Street, Sunday in the park, City Hall, a place of worship, the friendship circle at camp.

Design for interaction. Allowing for flexibility, for unanticipated uses. Exploring multiple uses of space, indoors or outdoors, to expand the program possibilities. Extending the public realm, making room for culture, for public functions in private spaces. For Mithun, understanding community begins with understanding culture, with demographics, GIS data, and stakeholder workshops – with asking and listening respectfully, inspiration. First and foremost, it says "Welcome": bringing youth and elders together, something designed to last, influencing future generations, being part of something bigger.

CHAPTER 8: LLOYD CROSSING

INTRODUCTION

A GLIMPSE OF TOMORROW'S CITYSCAPE

"Let us ask the land where are the best sites. Let us establish criteria for many different types of excellence responding to a wide range of choice."
Ian McHarg, Design With Nature

"Most urban planning still assumes the continuance of large scale, inflexible, separate utilities. Lloyd Crossing looks ahead to a future in which 21st century urban habitat, water and energy systems are closely interconnected. It then goes beyond traditional green building-level strategies to implement block- and neighborhood-wide sustainable systems and infrastructure."

—Bert Gregory, FAIA, Mithun

Someday, the words "Lloyd Crossing" may be held up as the first, best example of a true urban ecosystem, a place synonymous with healthy urban living that incorporates a diverse mix of uses and convenient transportation connections.

A sustainable neighborhood conceived and defined by Mithun, Lloyd Crossing is a real place: an inner-city section of thirty-five blocks near downtown Portland. As envisioned in the Lloyd Crossing Sustainable Urban Design Plan, the district could support a five-fold increase in development and quadruple its population by the year 2050. Through careful choices about open space and infrastructure, Lloyd Crossing could also reduce its water, energy, habitat and carbon dioxide footprints to pre-development levels – levels that existed when the site was a pristine forest.

This transforming of place was so powerful, in fact, that the plan earned recognition as one of AIA's "Top Ten Green Projects" of 2005 as well as winning honor awards from the American Society of Landscape Architects and EDRA (Environmental Design Research Association).

"Design must imagine and discern, assume,
purpose and attempt articulation, in as
synergetic a manner as possible."

—*Buckminster Fuller, Ideas and Integrities*

LLOYD CROSSING SUSTAINABLE
URBAN DESIGN PLAN
Portland, Oregon

The Lloyd Crossing Plan articulates the vision, goals and strategies necessary to establish
a sustainable framework and identity for an urban neighborhood. Rather than laying
environmental objectives over the planning process, the plan began with sustainability as its
primary goal. Further, it establishes a methodology for benchmarking and measuring habitat,
water and energy use, and for modeling an urban setting that mimics natural systems.

Named for its location at the nexus of Portland's light-rail and a planned streetcar line, the
Lloyd Crossing area is dramatically underutilized. Mithun's design challenge: how to turn
the neighborhood into a vibrant, attractive and highly desirable place to live and work, while
simultaneously reducing its net environmental impact over time.

Lloyd Crossing as an ideal is perhaps most significant for its transferability to other urban
settings. This neighborhood strategy elevates the sustainable planning of individual buildings
to include campus planning, institutions, neighborhoods – even cities and entire regions.
Portland intends to adopt this model throughout the city, scaling the details up or down
to suit other locations and applications. Already, the concept is generating interest from
planners and far beyond the Northwest.

DESIGN OVERVIEW

The Lloyd Crossing Plan began with a novel premise: that it may be possible to increase urban
density, expand wildlife habitat and connections to the larger landscape, to live within a site's
rainfall and solar budgets, and achieve carbon balance – all while developing renewable wind
and solar energy systems to ensure that these improvements are self supporting.

To address the often complex issues of designing within the urban "right of way", Mithun's
plan envisions a neighborhood built by both public and private dollars. It also demonstrates
how green building practices and technologies can generate efficiency savings to create
significant cash flows back into the project, advancing the community's sustainability goals.
Benefits to the community and public agencies include increased property values, reduced

DIVERSE, SUSTAINABLE, 24-HOUR CITIES: Existing transportation lines, utility infrastructure, stable commercial tenants, and strong residential and commercial development potential make this an ideal district for growth within the city. It may also serve as a testing ground, a blueprint, for the future of urban life.

1 vertical axis wind turbines
2 vegetated roof
3 solar shading
4 cafe / living machine
5 solar control at south façade
6 photovoltaic or solar hot water panels
7 rainwater storage (opt.)
8 district thermal loop connect to building
9 to subsurface irrigation at landscape areas
10 district thermal loop connect to lloyd center tower
11 catalyst project

Wastewater
Reclaimed Water
Rainwater Collection

SUSTAINABLE PREMISE: The Lloyd Crossing Sustainable Urban Design Plan proposes a development of 10 million square feet designed to be carbon neutral and live within the site's solar and water (rainfall) budget. Individual properties and the public realm function together – managing to provide returns from shared resource systems that advance the development's sustainable goals.

demand on infrastructure, and increased resource capacity.

Another challenge was to create integrated habitat plans for an urban district, featuring enhanced open space and landscaped streets. Mithun's designers engaged in extensive research on sustainable urban development and found few precedents for this work. For example, optimizing conditions and design parameters for a "steady state" urban wildlife population is a concept that has not yet been fully tested.

To provide benchmarks for future sustainable development, the design team also introduced "pre-development metrics" in the district. They chose to use key measurements of ecological performance for the native mixed-conifer forest that existed two hundred years ago on the site. Further, the plan identifies resource strategies within the study area to address tree cover, precipitation and water flows, solar energy input, and release of oxygen.

Finally, a key element of the plan is the Catalyst Project, conceived by Mithun as a series of four tangible alternatives for the site's development that creates the backbone of the sustainable neighborhood.

INTEGRATED DESIGN PROCESS
The plan's origins lay in Portland's 2001 city-wide objectives for green development, which identified mobility, activity and livability as key principles to guide major public and private decisions. The Portland Development Commission (PDC) pictured the Lloyd District as a vibrant mixed-use urban neighborhood with high density, a distinct identity, and a variety of transportation options.

THE CATALYST PROJECT
Mithun was also commissioned to develop the conceptual design for the Lloyd Crossing Signature Project (the Catalyst Project), a mixed-use development that incorporates many of the concepts and strategies outlined in the plan for open space, habitat, water and energy. First and foremost, this project is intended to serve as a successful example of visionary sustainable planning and design for the study area and to encourage private investment in this central core neighborhood.

Public improvements anticipated for the Catalyst Project include acquisition and development of a one-acre public park, implementation of streetscape improvements in selected areas, the introduction of stormwater bioswales and mid-block conifer forest "patches", and replacement of displaced on-street parking with an underground garage.

Design concepts have also been completed for mid-rise and high-rise development options. The building program for the mid-rise alternative consists of one hundred-fifty residential units in two separate structures of approximately seventy-five units each, while the high-rise alternatives range from two hundred-forty to three hundred units. LEED® Platinum is a major goal for these structures: utilizing a variety of sustainable strategies to exceed the energy performance of existing buildings in the study area by at least a factor of three.

SOLAR STRATEGY: The Lloyd Crossing Plan's energy vision includes greater utilization of available solar energy and other renewable sources, generating cost savings for reinvestment in other areas. The total incident solar budget for the 35-block study area is approximately 161 million kWh per year.

100% **Solar Energy Input**
161,006,000 kWh/yr

95% **Solar Energy Reflected, Absorbed & Released**
152,956,000 kWh/yr

O2 Released
495.4 tons/yr

CO2 Used
681.2 tons/yr

Carbon Fixed
185.8 tons/yr

4.5% **Solar Energy Used by Photosynthesis**
8,050,000 kWh/yr

Carbon Balance
Net removal from atmosphere: 681.2 tons/yr

"Lloyd Crossing may serve as a blueprint remedy for all cities faced with rising air- and water-quality standards, rapid urban development, and the need for more power production and water-treatment plants. Though the plan includes a stand-alone demonstration project, most of the proposed changes reach for the future without breaking with the past."

—"A Green Blueprint", Metropolis Magazine [1]

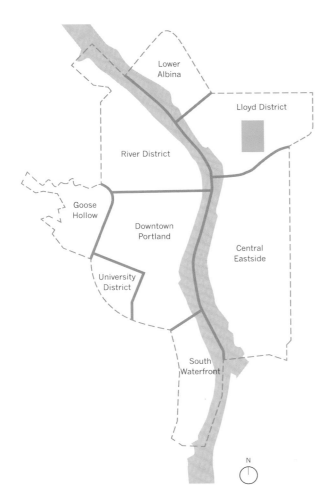

The PDC then sponsored the Lloyd Crossing study to examine the benefits of integrating urban design strategies, green infrastructure opportunities and shared building systems within this thirty-five block area as a model for the rest of the city.

Because the plan addresses very broad social, environmental and economic goals, it required deep research and input from an unusually wide range of disciplines. The initial design charrette brought together the entire consultant team, including specialists in real estate, landscape architecture, urban design, civil and mechanical engineering, and construction, as well as some of the region's top experts in neighborhood energy analysis, marketing and branding, and finance. As the group leader, Mithun was tasked with looking beyond conventional assumptions about urban development. Mithun focused on a future in which 21st century urban habitat, water and energy systems are closely interconnected, with block-and neighborhood-wide sustainable systems and infrastructure.

The vision for the Lloyd Crossing Plan was refined through a series of interviews, meetings, background research and collaborative work sessions. A Technical Advisory Group (TAG) brought together diverse city agencies to coordinate water, stormwater, energy, streetscape and other infrastructure elements within the public right of way. PDC and the design team worked with a stakeholder group of neighborhood residents, landowners, businesses and utilities to create early "buy-in" to the complex process of resource-integrated urban design. The resulting monthly forums provided valuable feedback to the consultant team.

Another critical step in the process was integrating environmental

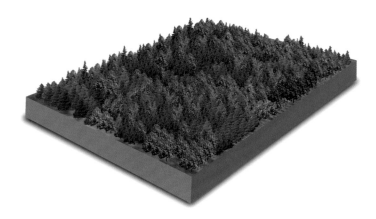

PRISTINE FOREST: A fundamental goal for the district is restoring habitat to nearly 100 percent of its pre-development conditions by 2050 – reducing net energy and water consumption levels to that of a patch of native Northwest forest. Habitat and tree-cover strategies, including green streets, wildlife corridors and bioswales, would combine to form an integrated urban streetscape.

metrics with financial payback and urban design elements. New, expressive forms were created for intersections, and wastewater treatment became part of the central urban space. The diverse, interdisciplinary team helped to create a culture of collaboration and learning, challenging each team member to expand their notions of design beyond buildings, streets and landscape to public policy framework, utility infrastructure, energy systems, habitat, and transportation needs. The green building concept was stretched and expanded to encompass "green neighborhoods."

THE SITE

The Lloyd Crossing neighborhood sits just behind Lloyd Center, an area passed over by the celebrated redevelopment boom of downtown Portland. Home to the Rose Garden Arena, the Portland Convention Center and Lloyd Center Mall, the district is bordered by couplets and ring roads that provide convenient auto access but create boundaries between the district and adjacent neighborhoods. It contains 176 dwelling units, offices for more than five thousand workers, and the MAX light rail line, which connects the city center and suburbs.

The plan's vision is to add eight million square feet of development over a period of forty-two years to the neighborhood, which is already well served by utility infrastructure with existing water, sewer, gas and power lines. The plan also recommends a combination of strategies for street-level and upper-level land use, street hierarchy, open space, landscape and habitat, ground-level building character, and tower setback requirements to create a more vibrant, attractive urban neighborhood.

As designed, habitat strategies weave a small, mixed-conifer forest

A VISION OF URBAN SUSTAINABILITY

The Lloyd Crossing Sustainable Urban Design Plan introduced the concept of a dense urban ecosystem to Portland's Lloyd District – suggesting "pre-development metrics" as a baseline for quantifying development strategies. Mithun and the design team outlined methodologies for achieving these conditions (as a pristine Northwest forest): restoring habitat levels for fish, birds and mammals; implementing water-neutral and carbon-neutral resource strategies; and developing energy systems and schemes that increase the use of renewable energy sources.

VISION AND GOALS

HABITAT
Restore pre-development habitat metrics through on-site and off-site strategies.

WATER
Achieve a "water-neutral" study area functioning within the rainfall budget falling on the site.

ENERGY
Live within the study area's usable annual solar budget and achieve a "carbon-neutral" study area.

DEVELOPMENT
Achieve the maximum allowable development potential in the study area as measured by allowable floor area ratio (FAR).

KEY URBAN DESIGN STRATEGIES INCLUDED:

HABITAT: restore habitat and tree cover by integrating a mixed-conifer forest into the urban streetscape – through the use of a hierarchical system of green streets, pedestrian streets, bioswales and public open space. Small-scale habitat corridors connect to habitat "islands" within the master plan area.

WATER: live within the site's rainfall budget (of 64 million gallons per year) by employing a water use strategy that results in 30 percent water conservation through use of efficient fixtures and provides 100 percent of non-potable water supply through rainwater harvesting and black water reuse by the year 2050.

ENERGY: live within the site's solar budget by creating a neighborhood in which the carbon balance and the use of incident solar energy match as closely as possible (and ultimately improve upon) pre-development conditions. This goal would be accomplished through building efficiency upgrades, thermal transfer between buildings, use of renewable energy, and purchase of carbon and wind offset credits.

PLACEMAKING: preserve urban density through a combination of strategies for street-level and upper-level land use, street hierarchy, open space, landscape and habitat, ground-level building character, and tower setback requirements that would contribute to the development of a vibrant, attractive urban neighborhood.

MATERIALS: achieve carbon balance through a process of evaluating and selecting construction materials based on long-term energy efficiency and low embodied CO_2 content, contributing to the goal of a carbon-neutral study area.

THIRTY FIVE BLOCKS: Home to the Rose Garden Arena, the Portland Convention Center and Lloyd Center Mall, this thirty-five block study area is cut off from adjacent neighborhoods and the rest of the city. Mithun's 54-acre master plan anticipates adding a mix of residential, office and commercial development over the next forty-two years while lowering the area's environmental impact.

into the urban infrastructure over the course of the development period. Overall tree cover would increase from 14.5 percent to 25 to 30 percent by 2050. Another fifty acres of forest habitat would be restored off-site at the adjoining Sullivan's Gulch. Two acres of mixed-conifer forest "patches" would be developed in the district, with an additional one to two acres of habitat corridor between these patches and the Gulch.

STRUCTURE & MATERIALS

The plan specifies construction materials based on long-term energy efficiency and low embodied CO_2 content, contributing to the goal of a carbon-neutral neighborhood. It is also anticipated that buildings in the study area would exceed LEED® Platinum-level requirements.

ENERGY

Lloyd Crossing's energy vision is to achieve a carbon balance and use of incident solar energy for the neighborhood equal to or exceeding pre-development environmental conditions. Load reduction strategies include: appliances and furnishings with superior energy efficiency; automatic controls for plug loads; water-efficient hot water plumbing systems; solid-state elevator drives with "smart" car controls; and variable-load controllers for escalators.

Planned photovoltaic and wind systems will represent the district's sustainable identity to the larger community. Renewable-energy strategies include: ten megawatts of photovoltaic (PV) capacity through rooftop systems, south-facing PV wall cladding, PV window shades for south-facing glazing, and PV arrays lining a three-quarter-mile stretch

of Sullivan's Gulch. Also, 1.4 megawatts of wind-turbine capacity are planned through two small (5 to 10 kilowatt) vertical-axis turbines on the roofs of high-rise office towers and two large (600 kilowatt) horizontal-axis turbines mounted on sixty-meter poles. Biogas will be generated from waste processing in the neighborhood. Additionally, the development will purchase wind power for 100 percent of imported electricity and carbon-offset credits for all imported natural gas.

HEATING & COOLING

The heating and cooling scheme for planned buildings relies heavily on bioclimatic design. Zoning will be modified to optimize solar exposure during build-out. The plan calls for detailed wind-flow and solar analysis of building massing and street exposure. Extensive natural ventilation and daylighting strategies will reduce the need for energy-intensive systems.

Buildings in the Catalyst Project respond directly to solar paths and wind patterns. The elliptical plan for the housing tower is designed to reduce perimeter area, optimize summer ventilation on the northwest axis, and use an offset elliptical solar screen to provide shading. The design also locates 75 percent of windows on south and west elevations for best solar access. Most apartments will have dual exposures to maximize daylighting and natural ventilation and cooling. Additional strategies include: optimal insulation levels in building envelopes; elimination of thermal bridging; high-performance glazing and window systems; and heavy reliance on thermal mass.

LIGHTING & DAYLIGHTING

The plan calls for daylight as the sole ambient light source, in

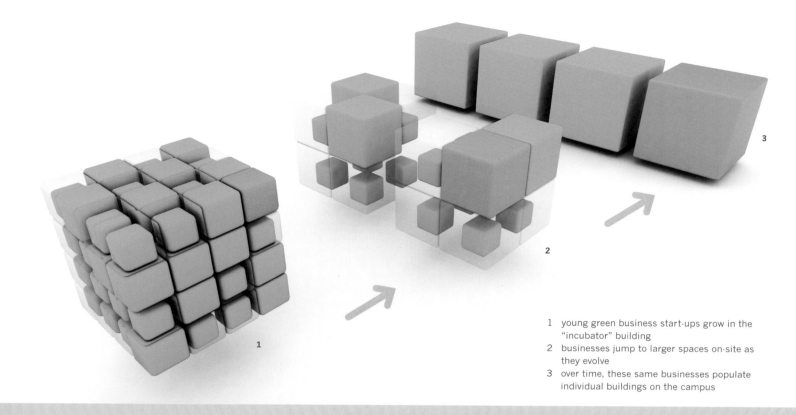

1 young green business start-ups grow in the "incubator" building
2 businesses jump to larger spaces on-site as they evolve
3 over time, these same businesses populate individual buildings on the campus

KITSAP SEED:
"A clean tech catalyst for change"

Kitsap County, southwest of Seattle, will soon be home to a world-class center for clean technology: a hub for energy research and manufacturing and an economic engine for the Puget Sound region. A Port of Bremerton initiative, the Kitsap SEED Project will become a business incubator for clean technology start-ups developing new products and processes to improve power generation, efficiency, storage, transmission, measurement and conservation. Even the buildings at this business park will serve as a showcase and test laboratory for the technologies of its tenant-partners: wind turbines, fuel cells, waste-to-energy systems and more.

This initiative is a story of jobs, of restored land, and an unprecedented display of sustainable design and technology. With conceptual design work and planning led by Mithun architects,

interior designers and landscape architects, the Kitsap SEED campus will evolve over time in phases, or modular "pods". Pod 1 will be the Clean Technology Commercialization Center, a high-quality office, laboratory and light manufacturing space. Net zero energy and water goals will be met through on-site renewable energy and on-site water collection, conservation and reuse. Mithun's integrated, zero impact approach to site development is designed to protect the surrounding habitat and watershed and achieve infiltration and evaporation/transpiration rates that mimic pre-development levels. And finally, the new center is aiming to be carbon neutral through co-located facilities, emerging solar technologies, green power and high energy efficiency.

1 porous concrete to maximize site stormwater infiltration
2 site stormwater collection and re-use
3 143 kw photovoltaic panel array
4 solar thermal collectors (22 kw energy contribution)
masonry shear cores provide daylighting, high thermal mass and stack-
5 aided natural cooling (fan assist)
6 structural insulated panel system
7 bioretention area collects excess roof stormwater to achieve 65/10/0 low
8 impact site stormwater strategy
9 operable windows provide natural cooling and daylight harvesting

10 high recycled content, low voc and regionally produced materials
11 FSC certified regional wood products
12 high fly ash content structural concrete
13 reclamation of former naval dumping facility site
14 radiant in-floor heating and free cooling
social gathering nodes encourage interaction and creative exchange
of ideas
15 geothermal heat exchangers
16 expressed building systems to enhance user awareness and
connection to resource use

Kitsap SEED (Sustainable Energy and Economic Development)
Project, Bremerton, Washington

LEED® Platinum (target)

Phase 1, 2009

24,000-square-foot building: two-story office/lab wing and high-
bay light manufacturing wing; 4.8-acre site

Building orientation optimized for active and passive solar
capture, structural insulated panel system, high thermal mass
shear walls create natural daylight wells & ventilation stacks,
operable windows, radiant in-floor heating and free cooling,
ground-source heat pumps, PV array, solar thermal (hot water)
collectors, bioretention area for excess roof storm water, site
storm water collection and re-use, high efficiency lighting, heat
recovery ventilation

"Kitsap SEED is a catalyst for future change. It's also a phenomenal
example of the integrated design process: reducing demand,
maximizing natural cooling and daylighting, geothermal, solar, solar
thermal, and low impact site development in terms of storm water
and the hydrologic cycle. The project is a true demonstration of
what's possible in terms of sustainable design."

—*Mike Fowler, AIA, Mithun*

50-YEAR METRICS: Defined by Mithun's design methodology, the plan establishes a baseline model for energy, carbon, water, habitat and specific development goals over a fifty year span. Metrics for each idea or strategy were developed for existing site conditions, predevelopment levels, and goals at a future date. "Pre-development metrics" measure the site's environmental performance characteristics in its natural or undeveloped state.

addition to ultra-high-efficiency linear fluorescent task lighting and "dark campus" (security tactic for campus surveillance) exterior-lighting controls.

INDOOR AIR

The Lloyd Crossing neighborhood planning concepts are designed to meet the highest possible environmental performance standards for indoor air quality and natural ventilation.

For the Catalyst Project, the narrow floor plates of the office tower take full advantage of cross ventilation, provide occupant views and optimize daylighting. The elliptical floor plate of the residential tower is oriented on a northwest axis to optimize wind speed and negative pressure at the exterior skin during summer months. Additional indoor-environment strategies include: three-fourths of all windows located on south and west elevations for solar access; residential building plan configuration allowing for dual exposures in most apartments to maximize daylighting and natural ventilation and cooling; façade design elements to create passive-solar shading; and daylight-sensing lighting controls utilized in all office areas.

WATER

To achieve its aggressive water conservation goals, the plan recommends a 30 percent reduction in potable water use through building efficiency upgrades and, by 2050, the treatment and reuse of rainwater and black water for all non-potable uses. These targets would reduce potable water demand in the neighborhood by 62 percent.

Water strategies within the Catalyst Project include dual systems for supplying potable and reclaimed water, individual rainwater-harvesting systems, and a shared black water treatment system to collect and treat all of the wastewater from the Catalyst Project and two existing office towers.

A proposed district-wide stormwater strategy would improve the quality of river water and reduce demand on Portland's combined stormwater/sewer system. It would also increase landscape and habitat areas (with indigenous vegetation), unify the streetscape design concept, and create a unique pedestrian experience. This design approach is intended to mimic pre-development watershed characteristics by using the natural flow of the site to capture and treat stormwater in a system of planted bioswales on the downhill side of each block and intersection. All stormwater generated from public rights-of-way would be treated and recharged into the ground. Additionally, on-site wastewater treatment systems would be integrated with landscape design.

ACCESS

Buildings will be constructed around the intersection of Portland's MAX light rail and a scheduled streetcar extension, creating maximum opportunity to use mass transit. Existing surface parking will be displaced by open space and future building development, as well as stormwater, streetscape and habitat strategies. The district's existing Transportation Management Association has focused efforts on improved public transit and ride sharing, bicycle and pedestrian measures, parking management and alternative work-hour programs.

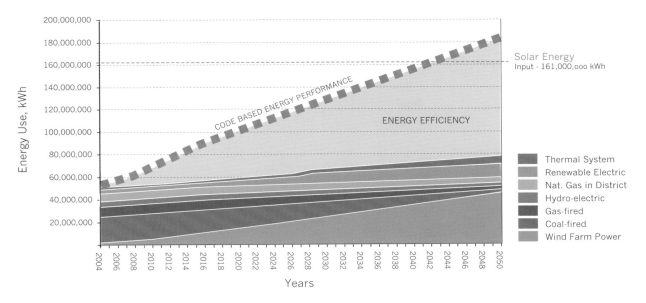

Solar Energy
Input · 161,000,000 kWh

ENERGY EFFICIENCY

CODE BASED ENERGY PERFORMANCE

Energy Use, kWh

Legend:
- Thermal System
- Renewable Electric
- Nat. Gas in District
- Hydro-electric
- Gas-fired
- Coal-fired
- Wind Farm Power

Years

ENERGY MIX TRANSITION

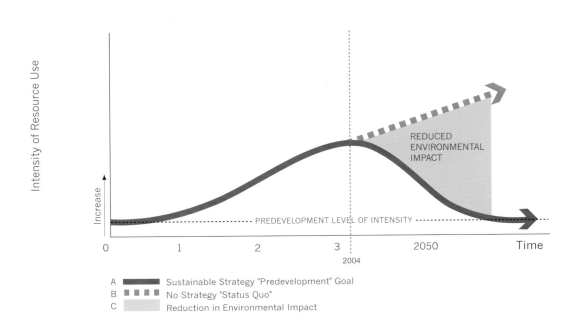

Intensity of Resource Use

Increase

REDUCED ENVIRONMENTAL IMPACT

PREDEVELOPMENT LEVEL OF INTENSITY

0   1   2   3   2050   Time

2004

A — Sustainable Strategy "Predevelopment" Goal
B — No Strategy "Status Quo"
C — Reduction in Environmental Impact

ENVIRONMENTAL IMPACT REDUCTION

THE CROSSING: Named for the future intersection of the MAX light rail line and a scheduled streetcar extension, the Lloyd Crossing Plan depicts a new transit-oriented development of towers and mid-rise buildings just across the river from downtown Portland.

CREATIVE FINANCING

Cost and financing mechanisms are treated as design elements in the plan, just as essential to the ultimate success of Lloyd Crossing as solar, wind or water strategies.

Central to this idea is another plan innovation: formation of a Resource Management Association (RMA), charged with creating, designing and financing district-wide green strategies and grant coordination. This new entity would implement sustainable development strategies throughout the district and manage Incremental savings from the high-performing energy and water systems to finance the capital costs for new green infrastructure. A percentage of savings would be returned to landowners to encourage private investment.

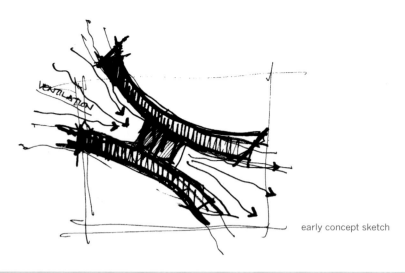

VENTILATION

early concept sketch

THINKING BEYOND THE BUILDING: The design team explored four separate high-rise building forms as part of the Lloyd Crossing Catalyst Project, each with different sustainable qualities: "Airstream", "Eclipse", "Solar Veil" and "Zephyr". The Airstream (pictured) shape is designed to capture summer breezes and features cross ventilation in units, optimal views toward the Willamette River, solar control through balconies, a rooftop garden, and rainwater collection.

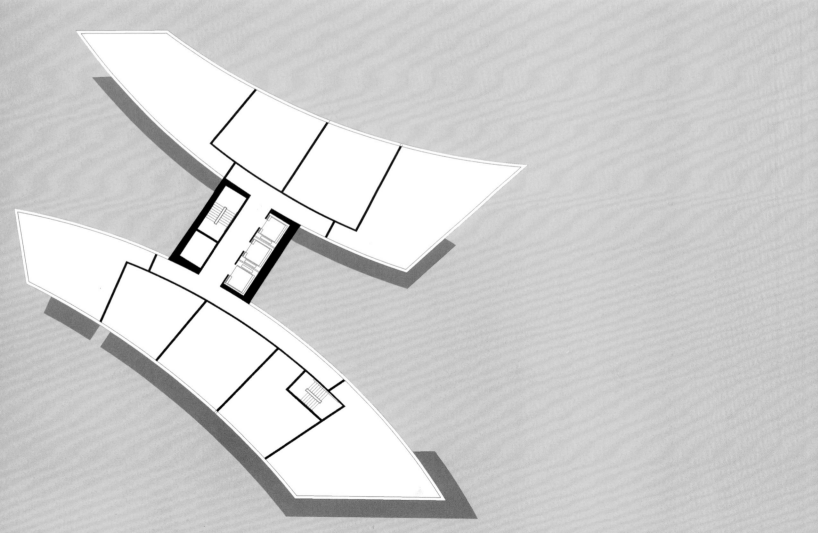

PRINCIPLE 7

BRING PASSION LEAVE EGO

TETON SCIENCE SCHOOLS

"Everything is revealed to you at once. Sited between the trees on the north-facing slope and sagebrush on the south, the campus architecture and landscape design had to respond to that simultaneous discovery. No one building stands out as an object in the valley; all are nested into their places as much as possible and yet clearly related."

—Brendan Connolly, AIA, Mithun

TETON SCIENCE SCHOOLS

Jackson, Wyoming

September 2005

"Cycle of the seasons, the rhythm of rituals"

At the end of the road, beyond 6,300 feet, the school appears: placed carefully along the narrow valley, respectful, blended, a part of the landscape. The buildings respond to natural site forces and topography – their roof planes aligned with the surrounding rock strata, their forms oriented to maximize daylight, passive solar gain and natural ventilation. The Jackson Campus of Teton Science Schools is a "land-learning lab", providing space for the pre-K through 12 Journeys School as well as overnight field experiences and conferences for adults and families. The welcome center, dining hall,

on less than 2 percent of the nearly nine hundred acres filled with creeks, ponds, aspen, conifer, grassland and sage habitats.

In creating the School's newest campus, Mithun designers sought to understand the valley's own rhythms – the annual cycles of birds and flowers, how elk and mule deer move through the valley – and weaving those into the school calendar. As a result, all of the one- and two-story buildings rest against the hillsides, full of light, taking advantage of late-day shading in summer, preserving wildlife corridors below and

To create a landscape that invites, an interior space that encourages interaction, a master plan that builds context and community. Places for people first, welcoming, accessible. Embracing "Bring Passion, Leave Ego" is an idea at the core of Mithun's own processes and people, the pursuit of deep green, affordable housing, sustainable development on a scale never attempted before. It may appear as buildings that are not buildings, that become an integral part of their surroundings. Through exploring the creative use of density in urban neighborhoods of the future. Or by envisioning an office with no walls: the democratic design of a movable, flexible workplace to foster communication and connectedness. A place where everyone shares the best views.

It is not about size, it is about people, personalities, families, children, lives. And as long as we stay focused on quality, we will continue to grow naturally as a firm. That is part of leaving ego at the door.

Compassionate and confident. Entrepreneurial but collaborative. Approachable design that is also visually and sculpturally compelling. Fresh, adaptive, responding to place: where no two projects look alike, perform alike, or even "think" alike.

Designer as integrator, mentor, student, partner – that is the Mithun way. Building relationships. A desire to learn. Forging new ground. Genuine design solutions. Leadership through listening. Seeking strong, visionary clients with shared values – clients who are passionate and demanding and deeply engaged as part of the design team.

CHAPTER 9: ISLANDWOOD

INTRODUCTION

"IslandWood was created to be an experiential place, designed so that each of its structures become a 'textbook', something the kids can operate. There, they can learn which direction is north, which direction is south; they can learn how the wind moves and how the sun moves; and they learn how to be better stewards of the environment."

— *David Goldberg, AIA, Mithun*

A LIGHT IN THE FOREST

"Children are the hands by which we take hold of heaven."
Henry Ward Beecher

At IslandWood – "A School in the Woods" – much of the learning happens beneath the trees, the towering Douglas firs and Western red cedars, surrounded by sword ferns, moss-covered logs and boulders, leaves littering the forest floor – the sound of birdsong across a meadow, wind moving through the alders, the smell of water and the earth.

Located across Puget Sound from Seattle, this private, non-profit center gives area school children the chance to experience the natural world. Outdoors, they explore science, mathematics, writing, technology, culture and the arts through the study of plants, wildlife or stream ecology. Inside, they interact with buildings that serve as showcases of sustainable design and construction.

IslandWood's most valuable lessons are those of transformation, discovery and surprise – what founder Debbi Brainerd originally envisioned as "a magical place for learning".

ISLANDWOOD

Bainbridge Island, Washington

Every week during the school year, approximately one hundred students, ages nine to twelve, spend four days and three nights at IslandWood with their teachers, exploring a nearly complete watershed of forest and wetlands. Once, the project's site was the center of a thriving logging operation, adjacent to the largest lumber mill in the world. A century later, this wooded setting provides immediate access to the natural and cultural history of Puget Sound.

IslandWood is a living laboratory for learning. In the midst of spectacular natural surroundings, it is the built environment that also teaches here. The classrooms are the shelters, bird blinds and other outdoor structures scattered throughout the site. Dormitories feature fireplaces made of Pacific Northwest stone. Rooftops have solar-panels. Building designs demonstrate the dynamics of air, temperature, light and water.

Completed in September 2002, IslandWood became Washington State's first LEED® Gold project. Now, after more than five years of operation, it is regarded as an international model for youth-based environmental education. The outdoor learning center now attracts four thousand schoolchildren annually from more than sixty schools and another four thousand adult visitors and volunteers for hosted conferences and community events.

DESIGN OVERVIEW

Mithun recommended the new campus pursue LEED® certification for its main structures—through strategies to maximize energy efficiency, minimize building footprints, keep materials out of the waste stream, use materials efficiently, and emphasize recycled content. The client and project team agreed that IslandWood's overarching design intent should include the following:

- Protection of the entire property through environmentally-intelligent design
- Best practices in environmental education for a state-of-the-art facility
- Buildings that function as interactive learning tools
- Connections to nature

SOLAR MEADOWS: An important feature of Island-Wood, solar meadows were carved out of the dense forest to allow direct sunlight into the buildings and maximize solar gain for the PV arrays atop the Learning Studios (classrooms). The Living Machine™ (right) serves as an on-site biological wastewater treatment plant and interactive aquatic science classroom.

LIVING MACHINE

FRIENDSHIP CIRCLE: A place to relive their experiences, to share their discoveries: school kids look forward to gathering at the Friendship Circle, a constructed forest amphitheater, on their final day at the center.

Sustainable land use planning began early with Brainerd and the design team working together to determine the best placement of buildings. Mithun identified potential locations through the use of aerial photographs, site visits and map overlays to highlight logged areas, steep slopes, suitable soils, and experiential features. In the final site layout, the center's structures are clustered on less than six acres of the 255-acre property – limiting development of the main campus to an area where the tree farm had last harvested in 1977.

IslandWood is an educational setting. Yet it is also a place where the buildings are designed to teach history, natural history and the principles of sustainability. Sculpture, found art, paintings, photographs and botanical prints can be found everywhere. Throughout the campus are handcrafted railings, furniture and fixtures built of wood harvested from the building sites. Classroom floors are laid with a variety of sustainable materials so students can learn about alternatives to wood; bathrooms have tiles made of recycled glass.

Visitors to IslandWood also learn first-hand how passive heating and cooling, water-efficient features, natural daylighting, and solar technologies reduce the center's electricity and water consumption by half. Guests shower in lodges with solar-heated water. They feel how the buildings' breathe through natural ventilation. They see the way in which the "butterfly roof" of the Learning Studios taps the sun's energy and diverts rainwater into a cistern. And they understand the workings of the Living Machine, an elaborate natural treatment system that purifies wastewater for irrigation and laundry uses.

The suggestions of schoolchildren had a profound impact on the design of lodges, the trail system and various outdoor field structures.

Children wanted to sleep out in the woods. They asked for reading lights by each bunk bed, windows so they could look out at trees, and private showers ("no outhouses"). The designers also recognized that children should be able to experience the entire property. The children's "wish lists" resulted in tree houses, bridges and watchtowers, shelters under the trees, and opportunities to explore the pond, streams and marsh.

INTEGRATED DESIGN PROCESS
The collaborative process to create IslandWood began with Seattle's Paul and Debbi Brainerd, who dreamed of ways to simultaneously address shortfalls in inner-city education and preserve the region's ecosystems. Soon after selling software developer Aldus Corp. (a firm Paul founded in the 1980s), they started the Brainerd Foundation. In 1997 the Brainerds put up $5 million to purchase a parcel of undeveloped land on Bainbridge Island. Their vision: that urban kids could learn about the natural and cultural history of the Puget Sound region if they could live in the forest for a short time.

Out of this vision was born the Puget Sound Environmental Learning Center, with Debbi as its executive director. Inspired by Mithun's work on the REI Seattle flagship store, she selected the firm to lead development of what was soon renamed IslandWood. In November 1998, Mithun's architects began their design process with a rainy overnight campout on the project site to gain a better sense of what students would experience. Brainerd and the designers also met with environmental educators, traveling to more than twenty-five existing outdoor education facilities across the country – sleeping in bunk beds, learning from naturalists, keeping journals, telling stories.

"Tug on anything at all and you'll find it connected to everything else in the universe."

—*John Muir*

Everyone agreed that children would be the project's true clients. So the design team collaborated with the University of Washington College of Architecture and Urban Planning to arrange a series of design charrettes with 250 fourth-, fifth- and sixth-graders over a period of six months. Children built models, answered questions about their favorite outdoor memories, made drawings of ideal spaces – and ultimately provided insights into what would be a safe, fun and engaging educational environment.

Two years of research, focus groups and community meetings involved more than twenty-five hundred people, including biologists, artists, educators, naturalists, cartographers, geologists, trail builders and cultural historians. As project leader, Mithun's role was vital in translating these ideas into building and site designs. Every design decision had to meet the team's bottom-line criteria for experience-based learning, sustainability and budget:

"Sometimes the interests of the children and the site were at odds. To overcome the difficulties this presented, the team adopted a detailed decision-making process. For example, as it looked at 15 different kinds of windows, the team tried to both create a woodsy experience and maintain the buildings' energy performance."[1]

Initial concerns about cost were balanced with the unprecedented opportunity at IslandWood to showcase sustainability visually in all aspects of the campus.

THE SITE
Carved out of the original eleven hundred-acre tree farm, the IslandWood property encompasses six different ecosystems. The

BACK TO NATURE: Once the site of a tree farm, and before that an extensive logging operation, the 255-acre campus hosts thousands of Seattle-area schoolchildren and adults annually. Visitors' first introduction to hands-on learning and sustainably-designed facilities at IslandWood is the Main Center: the Great Hall, Administration Office and Welcome Center, all certified LEED® Gold in 2002.

"An incredible experience for me, as an architect and parent, was having both of my sons participate in the IslandWood experience. My wife and I were chaperones for each of the children, and it was exciting to see the children's excitement over the entire environment that has been created at IslandWood, and enlightening to see how they actually used some of the learning spaces. Many of the outdoor and indoor circulation spaces became the 'classrooms' and confirmed that the quality of these spaces was important for creating an essential link between the indoor experience and being in the woods. The legacy of experiences that IslandWood creates has been the most powerful affirmation of the design process."

—*Richard Franko, AIA, Mithun*

forest consists of mostly second-growth Western red cedar, along with Douglas fir, big-leaf maple and alder. The watershed includes wetlands as well as a stream, pond, cattail marsh, bog and harbor. The bog is a rare habitat that features a stand of Western hemlock as well as Labrador tea, which thrives in the Arctic, and sundew, a carnivorous plant.

In the nineteenth century, this land was logged extensively to support the Port Blakely Mill, once the largest in the world. After the sawmill had gone out of business in the 1920s, the area was cleared in pockets over five decades as a stockpile for Port Blakely Tree Farms. When island logging became too expensive, the company chose to develop a massive housing project on the site – one of the island's last undeveloped parcels. That plan set off local protests until the property was acquired by the Brainerds.

THE PROGRAM
The campus totals seventy thousand square feet, with twenty-three buildings and sixteen outdoor structures spread over six acres of the property. IslandWood begins with the Welcome Shelter, just off the main parking area where buses drop off hundreds of students every week. Mithun established two paths into IslandWood, each designed to shape visitors' first impressions and point toward their experience to come.

The Main Center includes the Great Hall, Administration Office and the Welcome Center. The Great Hall is used to host meetings and conferences and serves as a gathering space for school kids during their stay. Adjoining this building is the Dining Hall, composed of the kitchen, restrooms and laundry operation. To the north is staff

housing and the Garden Classroom, which features the greenhouse, a garden for organic produce and herbs, and composting facilities.

Thirty yards to the east along the main trail is the Learning Studios building, containing seven classroom spaces under one roof. Across the main solar meadow is the "Living Machine", a tertiary treatment system for wastewater. Immediately south is the Creative Arts Studio, a non-traditional, artistic space nestled into the edge of the woods.

IslandWood's three Sleeping Lodges – the "Mammal's Den", the "Bird's Nest Lodge" and the "Invertebrate Inn" – are located approximately two hundred yards southeast of the main meadow and Welcome Center. Each building has its own loft and "Great Room," focused around a fireplace/stone chimney made of native rock. Designed to accommodate about one hundred-twenty students and teachers, the overnight lodges feature rooms with two sets of bunk beds, each with its own private toilet-sink-shower arrangement.

A network of pathways and trails leads to remote learning sites around IslandWood: the Tree House, sitting twenty-five feet up the bole of a Douglas fir, serves as a forest canopy classroom with a birds-eye view over the bog; a suspension footbridge stretches fifty-two feet above a forested ravine; and nearby, a floating platform effectively becomes a classroom on the pond. Not far from the lodges is the Friendship Circle, a constructed forest amphitheater where school groups meet for their final gatherings, a place to sum up their four days of experiences at the center.

Finally, IslandWood provides housing for University of Washington graduate students while they are earning their Master's in education

SIGHT, TOUCH, SMELL, FEEL, SOUND: Every detail and every space within the Learning Studios is designed to arouse childrens' curiosity about nature and sustainable materials. Classroom floors feature cork, bamboo, recycled rubber, and recycled-content concrete, while countertops are made of recycled-content concrete, recycled yogurt container composite, or soybean/sunflower seed bio-composite.

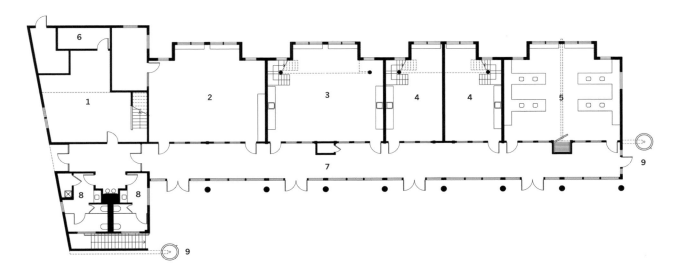

1 educational storage
2 technology studio
3 sustainability studio
4 ecosystem science studio
5 wetlands studio
6 photovoltaic controls
7 solar lobby
8 composting toilet room
9 rainwater cistern

TREE HOUSE: One of several remote site structures across the property, IslandWood's Tree House is a popular destination – high up a Douglas fir and overlooking a thousand-year-old bog.

or environmental science and teaching graduate-level classes. Located a half mile northwest of the Main Center, the grad complex includes eight cabins (two students per cabin) and a large garden plus the Commons House, which provides a kitchen, living area, study and laundry facilities.

BUILDING MATERIALS

Just as important to IslandWood's character as "buildings that teach" and maintaining a "deep-in-the-woods" feel are its product and material choices: salvaged, sustainably produced, locally harvested.

Design guidelines required that 5 percent of materials come from salvaged sources, that 20 percent contain at least 20 percent recycled content (as per LEED® guidelines), and 20 percent be manufactured within three hundred miles of the site. More than half of the wood products used in construction are from FSC-certified sources. In addition, all buildings were designed so that structural systems on the inside – including roof trusses and wood shear walls – are exposed, eliminating the need for finish materials. Concrete slabs contain 50 percent fly-ash in the cement to reduce the use of carbon-dioxide-producing Portland cement.

The campus's Welcome Center features recycled-content concrete and reclaimed wood flooring. Overhead is a 92-foot, 120-year-old salvaged wood beam suspended from the ceiling in tandem with a replica of one of the old mill's massive saw blades.

Each classroom within the Learning Studios has a different sustainable floor covering; countertops are made of recycled yogurt containers (from Germany), crushed sunflower shells, recycled concrete, or recycled soybean-shell bio-composite. Additional building features include recycled plastic toilet partitions, recycled-glass wall tiles, and 100 percent recycled cellulose insulation. Even the walk-off mats are made from recycled tires. Nearby, the straw bale walls of the Creative Arts Studio illustrate use of a natural building material.

The Sleeping Lodges feature recycled wood in their great rooms and lofts, cork flooring as a sound absorber upstairs, and throw rugs in bunkrooms woven from upholstery remnants and discarded clothing. Each of the lodge fireplaces – plus those in the Dining Hall and Main Center – represents a different time period in the geologic history of the Cascade Mountains: igneous, metamorphic or sedimentary.

ENERGY

Energy is essential as a teaching element within IslandWood's operations. During the design process, MEP consultant KEEN Engineering (now Stantec) conducted sophisticated thermal modeling to determine how campus buildings could be shaped and glazed to minimize heating and avoid air conditioning. Solar meadows were cleared around the buildings to maximize passive solar gain.

The 23-kilowatt photovoltaic array atop the Learning Studios provides half of the building's energy. For classrooms, the design team selected low-energy computers and monitors that consume one-third the power of the most common desktop computers. Additional roof area was included to accommodate the future installation of solar water heaters or more photovoltaic panels. Also, rooftop solar water heaters provide 50 percent of the hot water used in the Dining Hall and three lodges.

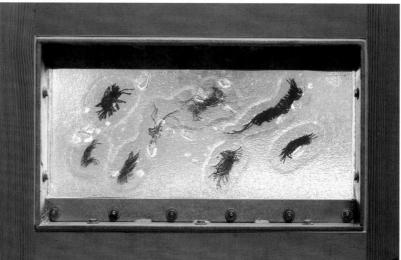

BIOPHILIC DESIGN: The principles of biophilia may be found in architecture and interior design throughout IslandWood: "Prospect and Refuge" (top) in the Sleeping Lodges, "Variations on a Theme" (middle) in the doors of the Creative Arts Studio, and "Serendipity" (bottom) in a copper sink within the Learning Studios.

"I told Paul, let's be proactive; let's combine our interest in the environment, education and children. Let's teach kids about the place they live so they understand it and make better decisions in the future."

—*Debbi Brainerd* [2]

The Garden Classroom and greenhouse feature both a micro hydro-generator and a micro wind turbine.

HEATING & COOLING

IslandWood's buildings were designed to operate primarily as passive spaces – encouraging visitors to think more deeply about their daily lifestyles and impacts on the environment. This design means functioning with wider-than-usual temperature "comfort zones" – slightly cooler in winter, slightly warmer in summer – than in traditional buildings. Building walls are insulated to R-19; ceilings are insulated to R-40.

Heat-dependent buildings are oriented along an east-west axis for maximum solar gain in the winter and overhangs on the south side to reduce summer heat gain. Strategically-placed windows trap the sun's rays inside for heat or allow cooling winds inside for ventilation. Operable awnings shade dining and office spaces. Two of the buildings were designed with butterfly roof sections to enhance natural ventilation. High-efficiency, in-floor hydronic heating supplements the passive design measures in primary buildings.

LIGHTING & DAYLIGHTING

All buildings are well daylit, with high ceilings and large windows offering extensive views outside. Open floor plans, oriented on an east-west axis, were designed to increase the amount of sunlight penetrating to the interior. Operable skylights further optimize daylighting and ventilation. T-5 fluorescent lamps with photocells supplement this light for offices and classrooms.

INDOOR AIR

Every building at IslandWood is naturally ventilated and includes operable, high-performance windows placed to maximize air circulation. Spot ventilation systems in bathrooms, kitchens and the auditorium control moisture and maintain safe indoor air quality. Small photovoltaic panels power building attic fans.

Buildings were also designed to minimize interior finishes. Where required, low-emission stains, paints, sealants and adhesives were used. Formaldehyde-free wood products were used in building interiors. To ensure the best possible IEQ, mechanical and electrical systems were commissioned prior to occupancy, and carbon dioxide sensors continually monitor air in primary spaces.

WATER

Native landscaping, rainwater collection and biological wastewater treatment all combine at IslandWood, not only reducing potable water consumption by 80 percent but also helping students to connect with and understand the hydrologic cycle. Bathrooms include low-flush toilets and waterless urinals, while composting toilets are located in the classroom building, in staff housing and at remote sites.

IslandWood treats all of its wastewater to tertiary standards so that no connection is necessary to the municipal sewage system. Subsurface-flow constructed wetlands are located near the sleeping lodges and graduate student housing. At the center of IslandWood is the Living Machine, housed in a greenhouse for educational purposes. This natural treatment center saves the center an estimated seventeen hundred-fifty gallons of water each day.

DEEP IN THE WOODS: The Learning Studios building (LEED® Gold) is bio-climatically responsive: windows open so interior spaces breathe naturally; skylights and tall north-facing windows provide optimal daylight; photovoltaic panels on the south-facing butterfly roof power 50 percent of lighting and electrical needs; and composting toilets eliminate water use.

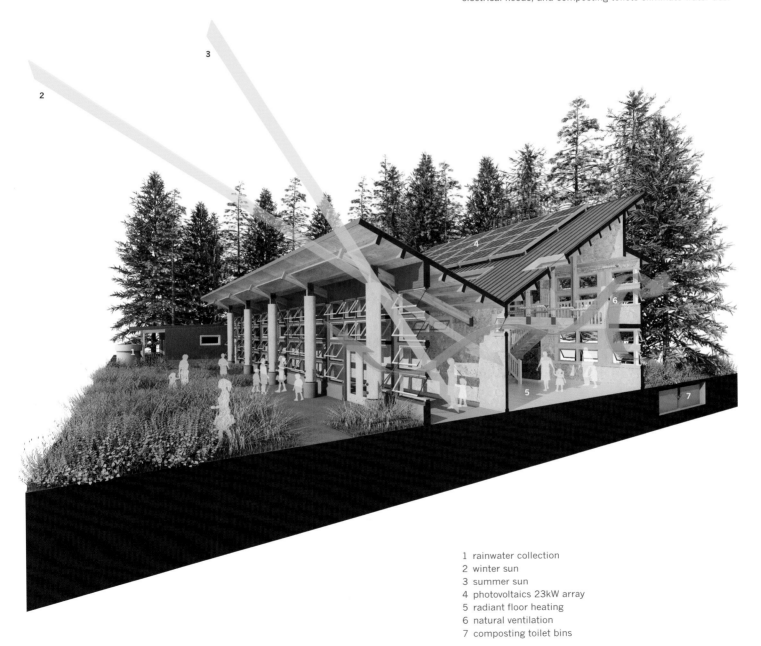

1 rainwater collection
2 winter sun
3 summer sun
4 photovoltaics 23kW array
5 radiant floor heating
6 natural ventilation
7 composting toilet bins

COMMISSIONED ART AT ISLANDWOOD

Bird's Nest Lodge	Eagle's Nest	Don Charles
Dining Hall	Food Waste Weigh Station ("Wade")	Peter Reiquam
Dining Hall	"Nin Pakidadjiwe", oil on linen and wood	Tom Uttech
Dining Hall	Tabletops (from dismantled Bainbridge Island barns)	Alan Vogel
Dining Hall Solar Meadow	Proposed outdoor music sculpture	Patrick Zentz (a Montana farmer)
Dining Hall, Lodges, and Admin Bldg	Railings, table bases (from recycled wood from site), settees, and arm chairs	David Kotz
Great Hall	House Post and carved and painted designs on the adzed posts	Roger Fernandes and Bruce Cook
Great Hall	Cedar bark panels	Subiyay Bruce Miller
Great Hall & Art Studio	Fused Glass Panels	Peter David
Great Hall and Welcome Center – Proposed	Interpretive documentation depicting the process of gathering and creating cattail mats	Yvonne Peterson
Large Conference Room	8 Botanical Prints, b & w photographs	Kari Blassfeldt
Library	"3 Seagulls and Water", b & w photograph	Mary Randlett
Lodges	Ceramic Tiles naming all rooms	Mette Hanson
Lodges	Morse chairs (made of certified Cherry, using the construction technique called mortise and tendon joinery	Ken Savage
Lodges and Admin Bldg.	Bunk beds, tables and chairs	John Lore, Pickle Ridge Furniture
Lodges and other bldgs.	Adirondack chairs (cedar from salvaged cedar from Olympic Peninsula)	Cecil Ross
Mud Room, Dining Hall; Main Bldgs.	Coat hooks (site-harvested Madrona), benches and door handles (Big Leaf maple and Madrona)	Erik Lindberg
Outside of Dining Hall	Fused Glass Tiles created by children	Diane Bonciolini and Greg Mesmer, Mesolini Glass Studio
Private Dining Room, Dining Hall	"Landscape with Stream", oil on canvas	Galen Hansen
Private Dining Room, Dining Hall	"Frogs" triptych	Roslyn Gayle Powell
Throughout campus area	Outdoor signage	James Bender
Throughout campus area – Proposed	Educational garden spaces	Lorna Jordan
Throughout Center	Fireplace Mantles (of madrona)	James Bender
Welcome Center	Mobius Saw Blade	Buster Simpson
Welcome Center	"Old Logging Gang", b & w photograph	Kinsey

LESSONS IN STONE: Each of the three Sleeping Lodges features a "geological" fireplace made with native rock – examples of buildings that teach, using art, space and architectural detail to create connections with the natural world.

Sedimentary

1 sandstone
2 fossils

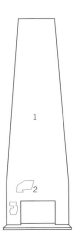

Igneous Stone

1 basalt seats
2 gabbro
3 granite
4 diorite

235

A WORLD AWAITS: Upon arriving at the Welcome Center, visitors are immersed in IslandWood's history, ecology and art – a preview to the rich variety of outdoor experiences that lay ahead. Suspended overhead is a 92-foot Douglas fir beam, thought to have been milled at Port Blakely in the late 1800s, encircled by the "Mobius Saw Blade".

APPENDIX I

PROJECT INFORMATION

REI SEATTLE FLAGSHIP
Seattle, Washington

PROJECT PROGRAM & STATS
Building Type: Retail
Size: Store is 98,000 square feet, constructed over a 160,000-square-foot parking garage
Stories: Two
Building Features:
- Retail space includes five outdoor specialty "shops" for Camping/Backpacking, Climbing/Mountaineering, Bicycling, Skiing/Snowboarding and Paddling.
- Also: office space, 250-seat auditorium, children's play area, art gallery, repair shop, rental shop and 100-seat café.
- Interactive features include a boot test trail, indoor rain room and Climbing Wall Enclosure, featuring a 65-foot climbing rock (the world's tallest freestanding indoor climbing structure).

Site Issues:
- Location in an emerging mixed-use neighborhood adjacent to the I-5 freeway and Seattle's central business district. Roof water is used to charge a waterfall that runs outside of the store, masking the sounds of the nearby highway.
- Store visitors enter the building through a native Northwest landscaped courtyard environment, which also serves as a neighborhood green space.

Completion Date: 1996

INTEGRATED DESIGN TEAM
Client: Recreational Equipment Inc. (REI) – Wally Smith, President and CEO

Mithun Design Team: B. Gregory (Project Director & Designer), P. Wanzer (Project Manager), R. Deering (Project Architect), K. Boyd, C. Huang, T. Emrich, K. Munizza (Interior Design Lead)
Design Consultants: Landscape Architecture: The Berger Partnership, P.S.; Structural: RSP/EQE; Civil: KPFF Consulting Engineers, Electrical Design: McKinney and Associates; Electrical

Design/Build: Madsen Electric and Cross Engineers; Mechanical Design/Build: MacDonald-Miller; Lighting Design: Candela

General Contractor: GLY Construction, Inc.

SELECTED AWARDS

1998
AIA/COTE Top Ten Green Projects, American Institute of Architects (AIA)/Committee on the Environment (COTE)

1997
AIA Northwest and Pacific Region Design Awards, American Institute of Architects (AIA), Northwest and Pacific Chapter, Honor Award

AGC Construction Excellence Award, Buildings over $10 million, Associated General Contractors (AGC)

Business Week/Architectural Record Awards, Private Sector, over $25 million

Architecture + Energy Awards, Design Award for Architectural Concepts and Materials, American Institute of Architects (AIA), Portland Chapter, Bonneville Power Administration, Portland General Electric

1996
ISP/VM+SD International Retail Store Design Awards, Institute of Store Planners (ISP) and Visual Merchandising and Store Design (VM+SD), 1996 Store of the Year

Honor Awards for Washington Architecture, American Institute of Architects (AIA), Seattle Chapter, Award of Merit

Chain Store Age Retail Store Awards, Environmental Design Integration, Grand Award

REI DENVER FLAGSHIP
Denver, Colorado

PROJECT PROGRAM & STATS
Location: Denver, Colorado
Building Type: Retail
Size: site, 5 acres; gross building area, 90,000 square feet
Stories: Three
Building Features:
- Used as a retail store as well as a restaurant and assembly space, REI Denver is housed in the historic 1901 Denver Tramway Power Company Building – listed in the U.S. Department of the Interior's National Register of Historic Places.
- Retail space includes five outdoor specialty "shops" for Camping/Backpacking, Climbing/Mountaineering, Bicycling, Skiing/Snowboarding and Paddling.
- Interactive areas feature a mountain bike trail, 45-foot-high climbing rock, kayaking course, and a cold chamber for testing and comparing recreational gear.

Site Issues:
- Located in a remediated brownfields area, near Denver's lower downtown district, at the confluence of Cherry Creek and the South Platte River
- The store's entry and public courtyard features a native Colorado landscape and high-efficiency subsurface irrigation system. Beneath the courtyard is a 40,000-square-foot underground parking garage.

Completion Date: April 2000
Cost: $34 million

INTEGRATED DESIGN TEAM

Client: Recreational Equipment Inc. (REI) – Wally Smith, President and CEO

Mithun Design Team: B. Gregory (Project Director & Designer), R. Deering (Project Manager), K. Boyd (Project Architect), C. Butler, L. McBride, J. Brown, C. King, C. Synnestvedt, C. Brookes, U. Bergk (Interior Design Lead), M. Saito

Design Consultants: Structural: Magnusson Klemencic Associates; Civil: Martin/Martin; Electrical: Cross Engineers; Mechanical: MacDonald-Miller Company; Historic Architecture: Semple Brown Roberts, PC; Landscape Architecture: Wenk Associates; Lighting Design: J. Miller & Associates

General Contractor: Hensel Phelps Construction Co.

SELECTED AWARDS

2002

ULI Award for Excellence, Small-Scale Rehabilitation, Urban Land Institute (ULI)

2001

AIA/COTE Top Ten Green Projects, American Institute of Architects (AIA)/Committee on the Environment (COTE)

National Preservation Honor Award, National Trust for Historic Preservation

Downtown Denver Award, Downtown Denver Partnership, Inc.

National Register of Historic Places

2000

ISP/VM+SD International Retail Store Design Awards, Specialty Store, Sales Area Over 10,000 sq. ft., Institute of Store Planners (ISP) and Visual Merchandising and Store Design (VM+SD), Award of Merit

State Honor Award, Colorado Preservation, Inc.

NORDHEIM COURT
Seattle, Washington

PROJECT PROGRAM & STATS
Location: Seattle, Washington
Building Type: Student Housing
Size: Site, 2.78 acres; 227,000 gross square footage for eight buildings
Stories: Mix of three, four and five stories
Building Features:
- 146 walk-up apartment units: four bedroom, two bedroom and studio layouts (total of 460 beds)
- Central plaza, smaller active and passive landscaped courtyards
- Shared tenant spaces: on-site fitness center, community room, laundry facilities, bike storage
- Below-ground parking structure

Site Issues:
- Immediately north of Seattle's University Village shopping center
- Previously the site of a commercial landscape nursery: legacy trees, mature habitat and man-made pond were preserved
- Apartment complex maintains easy access to public transportation and the Bert Gilman Trail

Completion Date: August 2003
Cost: Construction cost was $19.2 million
Ratings: LEED® Certified

INTEGRATED DESIGN TEAM
Client: University of Washington Housing and Food Service; Lorig

Associates, LLC (Project Management); Twenty-Fifth Avenue Properties, LLC

Mithun Design Team: V. Ferrese (Project Director), A. Hoyer (Project Manager), R. van der Veen and R. Gula (Project Designers), S. Williams, L. Malkasian, C. Tumanguil, D. Guenther (Landscape Architecture Lead), B. Yuen, T. Frick, M. Saito (Interior Design Lead)

Design Consultants: Civil: SvR Design Company; Structural: Perbix Bykonen; Electrical: Active Engineering; Mechanical: Key Engineering; Signage/Wayfinding: G. Scott Designworks, LLC; Art: Corson Studios LLC

General Contractor: Walsh Construction Co.

SELECTED AWARDS
2006
AIA Housing Committee Award, Multifamily Housing, American Institute of Architects (AIA), Honor Award

2005
Honor Awards for Washington Architecture, American Institute of Architecture (AIA), Seattle Chapter, Honor Award

2003
WASLA Professional Awards, American Society of Landscape Architects (ASLA), Washington Chapter, Honor Award

HIGH POINT

West Seattle, Washington

PROJECT PROGRAM & STATS

Location: West Seattle, Washington
Community Type: High Density, Mixed Use Housing Development
Size: 120 acres (34 city blocks)
Community Features:

- 1,700 low-income and market-rate homes, townhouses, condominiums and apartments; library, medical and dental clinic, neighborhood center; office/commercial space (10,000 gross square feet)
- HOPE VI Revitalization Project – one of the largest in the nation
- To protect water quality, High Point's engineered natural drainage system (NDS) is the largest in the U.S.
- Thirty-five "Breathe Easy" homes feature hardwood flooring and enhanced ventilation systems, weatherization and insulation to minimize humidity and moisture intrusion
- Twenty acres of open space, community garden spaces, market garden

Site Issues:

- Previously the site of a blighted World War II-era public housing project
- Master plan designed to reintegrate the neighborhood back into the surrounding West Seattle community
- Neighborhood comprises approximately 10 percent of one of Seattle's most productive salmon-bearing streams – threatened by pollutants and high volumes of storm water runoff
- Preservation of a large number of healthy legacy trees to help maintain habitat, community and site ecology

Completion Date: Early 2011
Cost: $133 million in total development costs
Ratings: BuiltGreen™ 3-Star certification or better for all home designs

INTEGRATED DESIGN TEAM

Client: Seattle Housing Authority

Mithun Design Team: B. Kreager (Project Director), B. Sullivan (Project Manager), M. Sullivan (Project Manager), S. Cox, T. Schacher, A. Hoyer, T. Johanson, T. Jordan-Oliver, B. Cloward, B. Bradford, D. O'Rourke
Planning and Landscape Architecture: L. Folkins (Planning Lead), R. Lloyd, B. Yuen, M. Harrison, K. Kirby, D. Guenther, S. Raab, C. Skipton, A. Bender

Design Consultants: Civil and Natural Drainage Systems: SvR Design Company; Landscape Architecture: Nakano Associates, LLC; Associate Architect (J. Calugas Apt. Bldg.): Streeter & Associates; Electrical: Travis Fitzmaurice, Inc.; Structural: PCS Structural Solutions; Mechanical: HV Engineering, Inc.

General Contractors: Phase One and Two: Absher Construction Co.; Sitework: Tri-State Construction; For Sale Home Developers: Lyle Homes; Saltaire Homes, LLC; Habitat for Humanity of Seattle and South King County

SELECTED AWARDS

2007
ULI Global Award for Excellence, Urban Land Institute (ULI)

ULI Award for Excellence – Americas, Urban Land Institute (ULI)
EPA 2007 National Award For Smart Growth Achievement, Built
    Projects, U.S. Environmental Protection Agency (EPA)
AIA/HUD Secretary's Award, Community Informed Design, American
    Institute of Architects (AIA) and the Office of the Secretary of the
    U.S. Department of Housing and Urban Development (HUD)
AIA Housing Committee Award, Multifamily, American Institute of
    Architects (AIA)
National Green Building Award, Multifamily Project of the Year,
    National Association of Home Builders (NAHB)
National Built Green™ Hammer Award (highest scoring community
    to date)
National Rudy Bruner Award for Urban Excellence, Silver Medalist
Gold Nugget Grand Award, Master Planned Community of the Year,
    Pacific Coast Builders Conference
Gold Nugget Grand Award, Best Infill, Redevelopment or Rehab Site
    Plan, Pacific Coast Builders Conference
Vision 2020 Award, Puget Sound Regional Council

2006
AIA "Show You're Green" Award, Excellence in Green and Affordable
    Housing, American Institute of Architects (AIA)
Energy Star Outstanding Achievement Award, U.S. Environmental
    Protection Agency and U.S. Department of Energy
Green Leaf Award, International Society of Arboriculturists
BuiltGreen™ Design Award, Master Builders Association of King and
    Snohomish Counties, Certificate of Merit

2005
Seattle BuiltGreen™ Design Competition, Communities Award,

Seattle Department of Planning and Development

2003
WASLA Professional Awards, Landscape Planning Award, American
    Society of Landscape Architects (ASLA), Washington Chapter
Master Plan Design Award, Seattle Design Commission

PSU EPLER HALL
Portland, Oregon

PROJECT PROGRAM & STATS
Location: Portland, Oregon
Building Type: Mixed Use, Student Housing
Size: 76,140 square feet
Stories: Six
Building Features:
- 130 Euro-style apartment units, 280 square feet each.
- Ground floor: classrooms, faculty offices, PSU Center for Science Education
- Top floor: "Global Village" themed residence life program
- Also includes shower facilities, changing areas and a bicycle cleaning station for biking commuters.
- Underground parking

Site Issues:
- Previously the site of a 1900-era apartment building and service station in PSU's student housing district downtown. All structures and underground storage tanks were removed and the contaminated soils remediated.
- Bordered by the Portland State campus to the east and north and by Interstate 405 on the south and west.

Completion Date: August 2003
Cost: $7.9 million
Ratings: LEED 2.1 Silver (first mixed-used LEED certified building in Portland)

INTEGRATED DESIGN TEAM
Client: Portland State University; College Housing Northwest

(Property Manager)

Mithun Design Team: R. van der Veen (Project Director & Designer), S. McDonald (Project Manager), R. Gula (Project Designer), S. Williams, S. Waytashek, M. Saito (Interior Design Lead)

Design Consultants: Structural/Civil: KPFF Consulting Engineers; Mechanical/Electrical: Interface Engineering; Landscape Architecture: Atlas Landscape Architecture

General Contractor: Walsh Construction Co.

SELECTED AWARDS
2006
Visionary, Technology & Innovation, American Society of Landscape Architects, Oregon Chapter, Merit Award

2005
Award for Stormwater Management, Businesses for an Environmentally Sustainable Tomorrow (BEST) Awards, City of Portland Office of Sustainable Development

2004
Pillars of the Industry Award, Best Student Housing Apartment Community, National Association of Home Builders (NAHB)
Excellence in Green Building Construction, Associated Builders and Contractors, Inc.

PIER 56
Seattle, Washington

PROJECT PROGRAM & STATS
Location: Seattle, Washington
Building Type: Mixed Use, Office, Retail
Size: 27,340 square feet
Stories: Two, plus a below-level parking structure
Building Features:
- Main office entry located on the building's north side is a separate two-story form, containing a stairwell and elevator.
- Open office plan features project-centric workstations, "Main Street" central walkway for design crits and public functions, centralized model shop and resource library, kitchen areas, and a common area at the west end for meetings and events.
- Mezzanine area for future growth and use as subtenant space.
- Semi-enclosed conference rooms named for annual Mithun study trips: Japan, Germany, France, Spain, England, Barcelona, Italy, Washington, DC.
- The building's eastern end (facing Alaskan Way) houses Elliott's Oyster House, the Argosy Cruise Line central office and staging area for departures, and a Simply Seattle souvenir stand.
Site Issues:
- Beams and columns on the southwest end of the building had to be rebuilt, a result of dry rot from continued exposure to salt water.
- Seismic bracing was required by city code – more challenging because the west end of the building was 10 inches out of plumb.
- Several pilings replaced with new steel pilings.

- Noise and air pollution from traffic on the Alaskan Way Viaduct just east of Pier 56 – a potential concern with operable windows/natural ventilation scheme.
Completion Date: April 2000
Cost: $1.5 million ($55/ft2)

INTEGRATED DESIGN TEAM
Client: Mithun, Inc.; Owner/Developer: Pier 55 and 56, LLC, represented by Martin Smith Inc.

Mithun Design Team: T. Emrich (Project Director & Manager), S. Bull (Project Designer), M. Anderson (Project Architect), T. Johanson, U. Bergk (Interior Design Lead)

MITHUN TENANT IMPROVEMENT
Design Consultants: Structural: Skilling Ward Magnusson Barkshire; Mechanical: Keen Engineering Co. Ltd.

General Contractor: Edifice Construction Co., Inc.

SHELL AND CORE
Architects: Design Architect: Mithun, Inc.; Architect of Record: Daly & Associates
Design Consultants: Structural: Coughlin Porter Lundeen; Electrical: Cochran Electric Co. Inc.; Mechanical Design/Build: Holaday-Parks, Inc.
General Contractor: J.R. Abbott Construction Inc.

SELECTED AWARDS

2002

What Makes It Green, American Institute of Architects (AIA), Seattle Chapter

Businesses for an Environmentally Sustainable Tomorrow (BEST) Sustainable Building Award, Business and Industry Resource Venture, City of Seattle

2001

January Project of the Month, American Institute of Architects (AIA), Seattle Chapter

Ten Shades of Green, Office of Sustainable Development, Cascadia Region, American Institute of Architects (AIA), Portland Chapter

2000

NAIOP Night of the Stars, National Association of Office and Industrial Properties (NAIOP), Finalist

LLOYD CROSSING
Portland, Oregon

PROJECT PROGRAM & STATS

Location: Portland, Oregon

Area: 35-block study area (inner-city, commercial) in the Lloyd District of Northeast Portland (54 acres, potential for 11 million square feet of development)

Scope: The plan lays out a new analytical, design and economic framework for adding 8 million square feet of mixed-use development over 45 years while dramatically improving the district's environmental performance. A four-block, mixed-use project, the Catalyst Project, will serve as a testing ground for key elements of the design plan.

Plan Features: By combining energy, water, habitat, place-making and economics, the plan targets the neighborhood to become a vibrant, sustainable, transit-oriented neighborhood:

- Public open space and restored habitat "patches" in streetscape environments that begin to re-establish and reconnect habitat corridors
- An increase in tree cover from 14.5 percent (2004) to 30 percent (by 2050)
- Integrated water system includes stormwater management and treatment, in addition to greywater and blackwater treatment and reuse for non-potable purposes
- Onsite renewable energy systems and resources such as wind power, photovoltaic systems and biogas generation
- A shared "thermal loop" system to balance heating loads among complementary uses

Site Issues:
- District – across the river from downtown – contains 2.8 million square feet of developed office, retail, residential and parking space, with intersecting transit connections, and undeveloped land
- Location of Portland's Rose Garden Arena, the Portland Convention Center and Lloyd Center Mall – isolated from adjacent neighborhoods by a series of couplets and ring roads; also bordered by the Willamette River to the west and on the south by I-84 (in Sullivan's Gulch)
- Typically occupied by 8,000 people, 112 hours per person per week, and 21,500 visitors per week

Plan Completion Date: July 2004
Ratings: Catalyst project modeled for LEED Platinum

INTEGRATED DESIGN TEAM

Client: Portland Development Commission

Mithun Design Team: B. Gregory (Project Director), R. Franko and J. Thomas (Project Managers), B. Kinnan, B. Ziegler, L. Copeland, R. Gula, R. van der Veen, M. Coates, K-H Liao, T. Meldrum, D. Pearse

Design Consultants: Civil: KPFF Consulting Engineers; Landscape Architecture: GreenWorks, PC; Energy Analysis: SolArc Architecture & Engineering, LLC; Real Estate and Financial Analysis: Heartland; Urban Design: Urbsworks, Inc.; Mechanical and Electrical: Interface Engineering; Identity: ID, Inc.; Cost Estimating: Walsh Construction Co.

SELECTED AWARDS

2006

Institute Honor Award for Regional and Urban Design, American Institute of Architects (AIA)

2005

Top Ten Green Projects, American Institute of Architects, Committee on the Environment (COTE), Special Recognition

ASLA Analysis and Planning Awards, American Society of Landscape Architects (ASLA), Award of Commendation

AIA Northwest & Pacific Region Design Award, American Institute of Architects (AIA), Northwest and Pacific Chapter, Award of Commendation

EDRA/Places Awards, Place Planning, Environmental Design Research Association

What Makes It Green, Sustainability: A Collaborative Process, American Institute of Architects, Seattle Chapter

2004

Honor Awards for Washington Architecture, American Institute of Architects, Seattle Chapter, Commendation Award

ISLANDWOOD
Bainbridge Island, Washington

PROJECT PROGRAM & STATS
Location: Bainbridge Island, Washington
Project Type: Residential Environmental Learning Center
Size: 255 acres; campus covers six acres, total building footprint of 70,600 square feet
Stories: Mix of one and two stories
Campus Features:
- Twenty-three buildings and sixteen outdoor structures include: Main Center (Great Hall, Administration Office and Welcome Center), Dining Hall, Creative Arts Studio, three Sleeping Lodges, Garden Classroom, and Graduate Housing
- 23-kilowatt photovoltaic array provides half of the classroom building's energy
- Rooftop solar water heaters supply half of the hot water used in the dining hall and three lodges
- Network of pathways and trails leads to remote learning site structures: tree house, suspension footbridge, floating platform on the pond, forest amphitheater
- "Living Machine", a tertiary treatment system for wastewater
- Subsurface-flow constructed wetlands located near the sleeping lodges and graduate student housing
Site Issues:
- Land was logged extensively in the nineteenth century, then became a tree farm operating until 1977
- IslandWood property encompasses six different ecosystems and a nearly complete watershed, including wetlands, stream, pond, cattail marsh, bog and other sensitive habitats
- Solar meadows sited around buildings to maximize passive solar gain
Completion Date: September 2002
Ratings: Washington State's first LEED® Gold project

INTEGRATED DESIGN TEAM
Client: IslandWood – Debbi and Paul Brainerd, Founders; The Warren Company (Owner's Rep)

Mithun Design Team: B. Gregory (Project Director), R. Franko (Project Manager), D. Goldberg (Project Designer), L. McBride, T. Rooks, A. Sturgeon, C. Kruger, B. Cloward, S. McNabb, J. Harrison, D. Swaab, K. Pirie, C. Dixon, T. Johanson, K. Tam, S. Martin, E. MacPherson (Interiors Lead), C. Schmidt, L. Herriot.

Design Consultants: Landscape Architecture and Planning: The Berger Partnership, P.S.; Planning: Bill Isley; Structural: Skilling Ward Magnusson Barkshire; Electrical: Hultz/BHU/Cross, Inc; Mechanical: Keen Engineering; Wastewater: 2020 Engineering, Inc.; Civil: Browne Engineering, Inc.

General Contractors: Educational Core: Rafn Company, Art Studio and Site Structures: Drury Construction Company; Graduate Cabins: Woodside Construction; Trails and Bridge: Sahale, LLC; Treehouse: Treehouse Workshop

SELECTED AWARDS
2007
IIDA/Metropolis Smart Environments Award, International Interior Design Association/Metropolis magazine

2005

AIA/CAE Design Award, American Institute of Architects/Committee on Architecture for Education (AIA/CAE), Merit Award

2003

IN Awards, Best of Competition, International Interior Design Association (IIDA), Washington State Chapter

DesignShare Awards for Innovative Learning Environments, Alternative Schools, Honor Award

Eagle of Excellence Award and Specialty Construction Award of Excellence, Associated Builders & Contractors of Western Washington

2002

AIA/COTE Top Ten Green Projects, American Institute of Architects/Committee on the Environment

What Makes It Green, American Institute of Architects (AIA), Seattle Chapter

International Design Resource Awards, Professionals, First Place

2001

Ten Shades of Green, American Institute of Architects (AIA), Portland Chapter, Cascadia Region

Craftsmanship Award, Construction Specifications Institute (CSI), Puget Sound Chapter

APPENDIX II

MITHUN SUGGESTED
READING LIST

A Sand County Almanac
Aldo Leopold Oxford University Press 1948

American Visions: *The Epic History of Art in America*
Robert Hughes, Knopf Publishing Group 1999

An Inconvenient Truth
Al Gore, Rodale 2006

Architecture of the Well-Tempered Environment
Reyner Banham, University of Chicago Press 1984

Biomimicry
Janine M. Benyus, William Morrow & Co. 1997

Biophilia
Edward O. Wilson, Harvard University Press 1986

Biophilic Design
Stephen Kellert, Judith Heerwagen and Martin L. Mador, Wiley & Sons 2008

Building for Life, Designing and Understanding the Human-Nature Connection
Stephen Kellert, University of Chicago Press 2005

Continuous Productive Urban Landscapes: Designing Urban Agriculture for Sustainable Cities
Andre Viljoen, Elsevier Science & Technology Books, 2005

Cradle to Cradle
William McDonough, Farrar, Straus and Giroux 2002

The Death and Life of Great American Cities
Jane Jacobs, Knopf Publishing Group 1992

Design of Cities
Edmund Bacon, Penguin Group 1976

Design with Nature
Ian L. McHarg, Wiley & Sons 1995

Ecological Design
Sim Van Der Ryn and Stuart Cohen, Island Press 1995

The Ecological Engineer, Volume One, KEEN Engineering
David Macaulay and Jason F. McLennan, Ecotone Publishing 2005

The Ecology of Commerce
Paul Hawken, Harper Collins 1994

Environmental Ethics, An Anthology
edited by Andrew Light and Holmes Rolston III, Wiley & Sons 2002

Fast Food Nation: The Dark Side of the All-American Meal
Eric Schlosser, Harper Collins 2005

Frank Lloyd Wright: An Autobiography
Frank Lloyd Wright, Pomegranate Art Books 2005

The Future of Life
E.O. Wilson, Knopf Publishing Group 2003

The Great Turning
David C. Korten, Stylus Publishing 2003

Health and Community Design: The Impacts of the Built Environment on Physical Activity
Lawrence D. Frank, Peter Engelke and Tom Schmid, University of Chicago Press 2003

The HOK Guidebook to Sustainable Design
Mary Ann Lazarus, Sandra Mendler and William Odell, Wiley & Sons 2005

Landscape Ecology Principles in Landscape Architecture and Land-Use Planning
Wenche Drumstad, James D Olson and Richard T. T. Forman, University of Chicago Press 1996

Last Child in the Woods
Richard Louv, Algonquin Books of Chapel Hill 2008

Louis I. Kahn: Complete works, 1935-74
Heinz Ronner, Westview Press 1977

Massive Change
Bruce Mau and the Institute without Borders, Phaidon Press 2004

Natural Capitalism
Paul Hawken, Amory Lovins, and Hunter Lovins, Little, Brown & Company 2000

The Omnivore's Dilemma
Michael Pollan, Viking Penguin 2007

Operating Manual for Spaceship Earth
R. Buckminster Fuller, Lars Muller Publishers 1969

Performance Art: From Futurism to the Present
RoseLee Goldberg, Thames & Hudson 2001

Performance: Live Art Since the '60s
RoseLee Goldberg, Thames & Hudson 2004

The Philosophy of Sustainable Design
Jason F. McLennan, Ecotone Publishing 2004

Women in Green
Kira Gould and Lance Hosey, Ecotone Publishing 2007

Zen Mind, Beginner's Mind
Shunryu Suzuki-roshi, Shambhala Publications 2005

APPENDIX III

ENDNOTES

CHAPTER ONE

1 Clair Enlow, "Mithun has arrived," *Seattle Daily Journal of Commerce*, 1990.

2 Brian Libby, "Environmental Intelligence Permeates the Work of Mithun Architects: A Firm Profile", BetterBricks.com. September 22, 2002.

CHAPTER TWO

1 "How Green Was My Company?" *Washington CEO Magazine*, June 2008.

CHAPTER THREE

1 "Terrestrial Ecosystem Responses to Global Change: A Research Strategy", J. S. Amthor et al., Publication No. 4821, Ecosystems Working Group, Environmental Services Division, Oak Ridge National Laboratory, Oak Ridge, Tennessee, September 1998.

CHAPTER FIVE

1 Neal Peirce, "High Point: Seattle's green community," The Seattle Times, Sunday, September 24, 2006 <http://seattletimes.nwsource.com/html/opinion/2003271360_peirce24.html>.

CHAPTER SIX

1 Marge O'Connor, "New Green On Campus: University Housing Proves Efficiency of Sustainable Design," *eco-structure*, January/February 2004.

2 Cathy Turner, *A First Year Evaluation of the Energy and Water Conservation of Stephen Epler Hall: Direct and Societal Savings*, Masters of Environmental Management Project, Department of Environmental Science and Resources, Portland State University, Final Report, March 16, 2005.

CHAPTER SEVEN

1 Edward O. Wilson, *Biophilia*, Cambridge, Massachusetts: Harvard University Press,1984.

2 Stephen R. Kellert, Judith Heerwagen, and Martin Mador, *Biophilic Design: The Theory, Science and Practice of Bringing Buildings to Life,* Hoboken, New Jersey: Wiley, February 2008.

CHAPTER EIGHT

1 Clair Enlow, "A Green Blueprint," *Metropolis Magazine*, July 25, 2005.

CHAPTER NINE

1 "IslandWood," In Depth Case Studies, Cascadia Region Green Building Council. http://casestudies.cascadiagbc.org/overview.cfm?ProjectID=497.

2 "From Tree Top To Bog Bottom", *Pacific Northwest, The Seattle Times Magazine*, Richard Seven, June 24, 2001

APPENDIX IV

PHOTO CREDITS

p 1   Bert Gregory, FAIA, Mithun
p 10   Chas. R. Pearson
p 12   Chas. R. Pearson
p 15   Chas. R. Pearson (top), Art Hupy, Photographer (center), Mithun (bottom)
p 16   Greg Krogstad, Photographer
p 17   Chris J. Roberts, Photographer (top), Doug J Scott, Photographer (bottom)
p 18   Courtesy of Mithun
p 21   Courtesy of Mithun
p 23   Lara Swimmer, Photographer (top & bottom)
p 24   Art Hupy, Photographer
p 28   Juan Hernandez, Mithun
p 31   Juan Hernandez, Mithun
p 33   Juan Hernandez, Mithun
p 34   Juan Hernandez, Mithun
p 36   Juan Hernandez, Mithun
p 38   Juan Hernandez, Mithun
p 41   Juan Hernandez, Mithun
p 42   Juan Hernandez, Mithun
p 44   Juan Hernandez, Mithun
p 46   Juan Hernandez, Mithun
p 48   Courtesy of Google
p 50   Juan Hernandez, Mithun
p 58   Courtesy of Aerotech Aerial Photography, Inc.
p 64   Juan Hernandez, Mithun
p 66   Juan Hernandez, Mithun
p 67   Juan Hernandez, Mithun

p 68   Robert Pisano, Photographer
p 71   Juan Hernandez, Mithun
p 72   Juan Hernandez, Mithun
p 74   Juan Hernandez, Mithun
p 75   Robert Pisano, Photographer
p 76   Juan Hernandez, Mithun
p 77   Juan Hernandez, Mithun
p 78   Robert Pisano, Photographer
p 79   Robert Pisano, Photographer
p 82   Juan Hernandez, Mithun
p 83   Juan Hernandez, Mithun
p 85   Juan Hernandez, Mithun (left, center & right)
p 86   Robert Pisano, Photographer
p 87   Courtesy of Forney Historic Transportation Museum
p 88   Courtesy of Forney Historic Transportation Museum
p 89   Scott Dressel Martin, Photographer
p 90   Robert Pisano, Photographer
p 93   Robert Pisano, Photographer
p 94   Robert Pisano, Photographer (top & bottom)
p 96   Eckert & Eckert Photography
p 98   Ryan Hawk, Woodland Park Zoo
p 100   Juan Hernandez, Mithun
p 101   Robert Pisano, Photographer
p 102   Doug J Scott, Photographer
p 105   Doug J Scott, Photographer
p 106   Juan Hernandez, Mithun
p 108   Courtesy of Seattle Housing Authority